Through My Private Eyes

David B. Smaha, PI LLC

ISBN: 1450576125

ISBN-13: 9781450576123

Library of Congress Control Number: 2010901848

DEDICATION

…to my colleague, teacher,
inspiration, role model,
best friend, best man…my Dad.
I miss you everyday.

ACKNOWLEDGEMENTS

So many people to extend my heartfelt thanks—so few trees.

Thanks to all my incredibly loyal and supportive clients throughout the years without whom my journey would never have been.

To my friends and neighbors, especially Jim Parisi and Kevin Cough who first listened to my stories and then encouraged me to convey my cocktail party stories in a book.

To my good friend, Rick 'the wizard' Charest for his patient assistance guiding this dinosaur through the computer jungle.

To my many colleagues but especially my two closest, Karen Serunian who never allowed a dull or silent moment during surveillances and Kevin O'Donovan, can you hear me now?...we had a blast. You always had my back..still do! You guys always made work seem fun.

Thanks to my self appointed volunteer staff of naggers. "How's your book coming?" You know who you are!

And finally and most importantly, my family. To my older brothers, Steve and Peter for leading the way and setting the bar so high I couldn't see it...so I found my own! And Peter, thanks for offering and sharing your amazing creative skills.

Mom, you instilled in me the belief and confidence that I could do anything yet kept me grounded with unforgettable advice like 'who in hell are you to think YOU deserve perfection'. Well, I may not deserve it but I got perfection with you as a Mom. Sarah and A.J., all bias aside, you two are the absolute best kids I could ever imagine in my wildest hopes and dreams. You give me a reason and make me proud every single moment of everyday of my life.

And my wife Renee...what can I say except that your consistent kindness and genuineness continue to amaze me through the years. You are unique. You are special. I so appreciate your never ending support, faith, understanding and true and pure love.

FOREWORD

As a state-licensed private investigator for more than twenty-eight years, I have worked thousands of cases, most of which were boring as hell. However, during those many years, I have been afforded the opportunity to investigate and become involved in cases that were anything but boring—cases that engaged me (*some* emotionally), cases from which I learned so much and saw so much… through my eyes…private eyes.

This book is a compilation of true case stories that individually and collectively convey a lot more than a story. From murder to lifelong lost love, my clients included high-ranking political figures, large corporations, the state, the United States of America, as well as ordinary people, likely no different than you.

While I hope and believe that these case stories are interesting (cocktail party tested in that regard), the years that have elapsed have helped me see things more clearly. I have come to truly appreciate the saying, "You can't see the forest for the trees."

One of the many things I have learned is that, eventually, most everything is sorted out and figured out. It is often not so much about "solving" a case as much as seeing the real underlying story—penetrating the deception to arrive at the truth of the matter. Years later, I now find it ironic that my philosophy in all my investigative work (whether interviewing, testifying, conducting surveillance, or training others) was "I just want to find the truth." I believe that justice is truth in action.

Well here is the truth, the whole truth...I look forward to sharing these case stories with you and hope that you not only enjoy them, but also take something away from them.

* * *

INTRODUCTION

You never know how quickly your life can take a turn!

I was in my early twenties when I became aware of a detective losing fingerprints in a burglary case involving someone close to me. I also learned that the lead police detective who lost the fingerprints extracted from the crime scene was a lifelong family friend of the key suspect in the case. Without those lost prints, there was no case against the key suspect, hence no charges. A classic case of "my buddy the cop getting me off"!

It bothered me so much. I lay in bed thinking, tossing, and turning. The next night was no better. The question resonated in my mind: *Where does it end?*

It's one thing for a cop to fix a speeding ticket for a friend. It's another thing when a cop "takes care of" a buddy who has committed a serious crime. If someone gets away with a criminal act, isn't it more likely, if not highly likely, that he or she will commit another crime after getting away with it the first time? That was my belief and fear.

Today it was a burglary, I thought. What may lie ahead for tomorrow? A sex crime, a violent crime? Why not? At some point, does someone who keeps getting away with wrongdoing feel above the law?

I felt compelled to do something but I had no idea what. My brother would tell me to get off my white horse and forget about it. My uncle, the judge, spoke out of the side of his mouth as he advised me just to "let it go."

My parents had instilled in me high morals and values. They also raised me to believe that I could do anything I set my mind to do. I knew the difference between right and wrong and what I had become aware of was wrong, very wrong.

I couldn't let it go so I embarked on a solo mission of justice. My carefully worded letter to *60 Minutes* would go unanswered!

I decided that I would go directly to the captain of the police department, the supervisor of the detective in question. Boy was I naïve and green! But where I was green and naïve, I made up for it with perseverance and balls.

The captain assured me that he was concerned about the situation and would immediately assign a new detective to resume the investigation into the original case. He would also turn the matter over to the Internal Affairs Department—the department that attempts to ascertain all your information in order to employ a cover-up that will defend the actions of their "law enforcement brother."

After a few weeks of hearing nothing, I made contact with the new detective handling the burglary case. He told me he could do nothing and that no arrest could be made. He was willing to keep the case open should further evidence become available. Then I determined that the Internal Affairs Department had completed their investigation and concluded that no wrongdoing had taken place.

I asked the Internal Affairs Department how they explained the fact that the detective who took the burglary case was actually a juvenile detective. In addition, there was irrefutable evidence that the detective who had requested the assignment knew the key suspect. Receiving no satisfactory response, my rage grew, which resulted in my being taken by the arm and forcibly led out of the police station. As I was escorted out, I blurted, "You think I'm done? You're wrong! You think this is over? I don't think so!"

The next day, I returned to the police station and asked to speak with the chief of police. I waited and waited patiently, but after nearly two hours, I had waited long enough. When the secretary stepped away from her desk, I walked down a long corridor and stuck my head into his doorway as the chief looked up from behind his big clear desk.

"Chief, I've been waiting two hours to see you. Could I please have just a few minutes of your time and I promise I'll go away?"

I think the idea of my "going away" appealed to him. He smiled and told me to come in and have a seat.

I explained to him what had occurred, giving him the sixty-second, highlights-only version. He looked me straight in the eyes as I spoke, but he didn't say a word or change his stern expression. When I was done, he told me that what I was saying was very serious and that he didn't take it lightly. He attempted to make me feel that he would get to the bottom of it.

Although I was young, I was growing up quickly. I didn't believe a word he said, but I understood why he was the chief. He was smooth and polished, but not good enough to shut me up or make me go away. That was the last time I spoke to the chief. Funny thing, he never called me.

I borrowed five thousand dollars from my dad and hired the very best attorney possible. The high-powered attorney must have liked the case because he was willing to take it on a contingency basis with me paying only for actual costs incurred along the way. We filed a federal lawsuit naming each individual involved as well as the police department and city as defendants.

The local newspaper picked up the story and published a large article that headlined in the "Local" section of the paper—"Federal Lawsuit Alleges Police Impropriety." The article sensationalized the suit and quoted most of the allegations contained within the lawsuit filing. I remember the satisfaction I felt the day the story hit the paper. I believed that I was doing the right thing in my effort to expose a wrongdoing—a wrongdoing committed by the same people our society entrusts to uphold the laws of our state and country. I believed that the guys who were supposed to do the right thing had grievously done the wrong thing and there was no way I was going to let it go unnoticed!

As is so common with our legal system, the process was extremely slow. To complicate matters further, I was told that the federal court docket was jammed and it was taking months just to get decisions on motions filed at hearings.

Lawyers took depositions of the key parties. The detective who had lost the fingerprint evidence was grilled. Under oath, he testified about his prior knowledge of the key suspect in the case. He testified that he vaguely knew of the man named as suspect because, as he put it, "It's a very small town sometimes." He referred to him as an acquaintance.

The attorney pounced on him, "Do you attend family reunions of your acquaintances? Do you give acquaintances nicknames? Do you refer to a close family friend as an acquaintance?" The detective became obviously flustered, red faced, and shaken. I sat across the table from him, enjoying every sweet second. We've got him, I thought to myself. I had already located a dozen witnesses who would refute his claims, including relatives of the suspect who told warmhearted stories about how close the two men were "their whole lives!" "They're like brothers" was a recurring theme among people that knew the men.

As time dragged on, I was fueled by the fantasy of a jury hearing the testimony that was being made clear through the slow-churning legal process.

In order to properly, accurately, and legally document evidence and witness statements, my attorney hired a private investigator. In light of the fact that I had already done a lot of related investigation, I ended up working closely with the PI.

A heavyweight law firm represented the police department and city. They were not taking this lightly.

The case dragged on. It had been nearly two years since the complaint was filed, but there was hope. A new judge had been assigned to the federal district and he had a no-nonsense reputation. He was known to get things moving. I felt optimistic again.

That was until I got one of those calls you never forget. The judge knew how to clean the docket all right. He proceeded to throw out cases by the dozen, citing obscure precedents and abstract technicalities. His strategy and motive were clear and, in my opinion, very unfair. He threw everything out, hoping that the matters would be resolved by the parties reaching a settlement or agreement rather than opting to go forward through a long appeal process.

It was big decision time. Even though the attorney was working on a contingency basis, meaning he would only get paid as a percentage of winnings, his advice was to attempt to negotiate. The appeal process could take years with no guarantee that the technicality would be overturned. I did some soul searching and authorized the attorney to sit down with the other side and try to hash it out.

I had to remember why I pursued this matter and I had to take solace that the outcome served my intended purpose.

The chief of police was moving on to a bigger municipality. That decision was not a result of this case in any way. It simply transpired during the two years that had elapsed. The captain of the Detective Division who would have been a leading candidate for the vacated chief position was forced to resign as part of the settlement agreement. And finally, the detective who was the initial perpetrator of the wrongdoing was terminated, a key and mandatory element of the settlement. In addition, the juvenile detective suffered a heart attack shortly after his deposition. Please note that he was grossly overweight, so the case was likely only a contributing factor to his medical problems. News of the heart attack served to enforce my core belief in karma.

I never got my day in court, but I believe that I injected a bit of justice that I hoped would have a positive ripple effect among many. I also forged a strong relationship with the PI with whom I worked on this case and I began to work for his firm. A few years later, the two partners of the investigation firm split and both solicited my employment in their new agencies. I struggled with the decision as to which one I would go with, and in an effort not to slight either, I began my own private investigation agency in 1984.

I vividly recall having dinner with my conservative dad, the greatest guy ever, when I told him about my career change. "Hey, Dad, I want to tell you something. I'm making a career change. I'm studying and working to become a licensed private investigator."

My dad dropped his fork onto his plate, stopped eating, and slowly turned his attention away from his thinly sliced London broil steak. He looked at me and said, "That's the most ridiculous thing I've ever heard and I don't want to hear another word about it."

That went well, I thought.

I will never ever forget the sound of Dad's fork hitting his plate.

* * *

CHAPTER 1

PEANUTS & CRACKER JACKS &...DAD

It was a beautiful spring day, a typical day in progress that just happened to be my birthday. I was sitting at my desk in the late afternoon feeling a bit reflective and a little sorry for myself having to work on my birthday. The reality was that birthdays just aren't what they used to be.

Then I heard a car turn into my parking lot, which was situated right outside my office window. Sure enough, dear old Dad was coming through. I couldn't contain a smile as I waved him in and motioned him to sit, all the while pretending to be interested in a telephone conversation. I was listening to some pathetic insurance claims adjuster bragging about his new strategy to settle workers compensation claims for employees out of work due to a workplace injury. He called it his "macaroni and cheese" plan. It was his plan to deny all benefits to claimants and effectuate a financial hardship on the out-of-work individual. With that in place, he continued, they would be able to afford only three-for-a-dollar boxes of macaroni and cheese. When claimants reached a point of wanting real food, he summarized with a chuckle, they would be forced back to work. By now, he was in full-fledged laughter.

Through his amusement, he asked me what I thought of his devious plan. I probably lowered myself to his level because I didn't tell him what I really thought. He was completely oblivious to his job responsibility. He just wanted to win. It didn't matter that people's lives were at stake. He believed that prevailing in a case where there was a legitimate injury served to balance the scales due to the fact that many fraudulent claims end up getting paid, often settled for sizeable amounts of money. It had nothing to do with what was right or how people's lives would be affected…it was about winning at any cost.

Anyway, back to Dad. He set down on my desk the shoebox-sized, funny-pages-wrapped gift, the same gift I had received from him every birthday for over a decade. All he needed to know was that I loved those top quality sirloin strip steaks he had specially cut to an inch and a half thickness (perfect cooked medium rare on the grill) to keep them coming year after year. No need to unwrap 'em, just a heartfelt thank you, a hug, and he was out of there. It was suddenly now a very happy birthday.

After Dad left, it was a lot easier to get into my work. In fact, I was absorbed in reading a package of discovery relating to a new court-appointed criminal matter when I received a call ironically appropriate to the moment.

The voice of the caller was noticeably uncomfortable, something that was more common than not. I had developed an ability to make those callers promptly feel at ease. The male caller asked some general questions about finding people and then revealed that he very much wanted to find his father. I asked the caller for his first name and then added, "Ben, let me try to help you. I'm pretty good at locating people and if I don't find your father, it won't cost you a dime." That did it. I had a new client. It was time to get started.

Ben was twenty-four years old and engaged to be married. It was one of the happiest times of his young life. As he told his mom about the news of his engagement and his desire to have children, he expressed his lifelong strong desire to know the truth about his father. His mother felt she owed it to him and was now willing to comply with his wishes, hoping and praying he would understand, forgive, and continue to love her.

Ben's mother, Rose, had raised him as a single parent. She explained to Ben that as a naïve and young nineteen-year-old, she had been engaged to an older man named Mark. She and Mark had a big blowout fight around the holidays one year and broke up. In the wake of feeling as if her life was falling apart, she had a brief relationship with a man who was in the navy and stationed at the Portsmouth Naval Shipyard in New Hampshire. She got pregnant, and by the time she found out, she and the navy guy were over. She tried to get back with Mark and things were OK for a while.

Rose explained that she felt obligated to at least tell the navy man that she was pregnant and that she was back with her fiancé, Mark. The navy man offered to pay for an abortion if that was what she wanted. It was against her belief system. Instead, she lived with this secret, hoping that Mark may accept the baby, especially if the real biological father was completely out of the picture. Rose explained this to Frank, the navy nuclear submarine engineer, who understood and wished her love and blessings in her life. Rose and Frank never spoke again.

Rose miscalculated her fiancé's acceptance of the news of the baby and that ended that.

After fourteen years of "doing the best she could" as a single mom and dealing with Ben as a teenager, Rose met a man and they fell in love. They had two children together and had a seemingly happy life. The new guy, Hal, didn't get along with Ben at all. In fact, it was downright ugly. Ben felt, and justifiably so, he was just in the way of the new happy family. He decided to go away to a private high school and Hal was thrilled. Even Rose thought it was best for Ben given the circumstances. The years passed but it always felt like there were underlying unresolved issues.

When Ben decided to find Frank, he told his mom and they hugged and cried. He loved her with his entirety and appreciated how hard she worked to give him the best life she possibly could provide. But it was time for Ben to do what he always wanted to do—find his biological father. He explained to his mother that because he and his fiancé had hopes and dreams of having children that it was important to know genetic history. Rose was not opposed to Ben wanting to locate his biological father; however, she was able to offer only very limited information. She knew his name, Frank Crosby, but not his middle name or initial. She also knew that he had been in the navy, stationed in New Hampshire, in the late 1980s. She smiled through her tears when she told him that Frank was tall and handsome just like her wonderful son.

Ben admitted to me that he had become obsessed with finding Frank Crosby but was unsuccessful with anything he had attempted. I explained that there was very little to go on; nonetheless, I believed I could locate his father. The price for my services was simple. If I locate your father, you pay me four hundred dollars. If I don't find him, you don't pay a dime.

Without a second of hesitation, Ben responded, "Deal!"

I got contact information for Ben and hung up the phone. After opening a file for this matter and organizing my brief set of notes taken during the call, I resumed my work on other matters. This was too easy, I thought to myself. After a good day of billable time, I didn't need to nail this one down right away to feel like I was doing all right. I also didn't want to take my best shot late in the day at the most likely source that could get me my information with a few computer clicks. If I were to catch her as she was heading out for the day, I was highly less likely to get full-bore cooperation.

The next day, shortly after 10:00 a.m., I placed a telephone call to a naval air station employee, whom I had met about six months earlier. Lori was what I would refer to as an information source in training. I had met her as a friend of a friend and had been in her company only a few times. Recognizing the potential, I had made friends with her and had joked about calling her when I needed top-secret military information. She had expressed a willingness to help me anytime, if she could. I had filed that "willingness" and was now calling in the offer.

I got her voice mail and simply asked her to call me when she had a confidential minute. I found that people loved the idea of returning a call that required confidentiality!

By the time Lori returned my telephone call, I had revised my pretext story several times. I thought the simpler the better. I told her that I was trying to do my father a favor. He was looking for an old friend of his who was stationed at the Portsmouth Naval Shipyard in the mid 1980s. I also let her know that I didn't want to get her in any kind of trouble and I assured her that I would never tell anybody where or how I got the contact information.

Without pausing, I asked her if she could give me a current address for Frank Crosby. She responded that as long as I didn't say anything, she didn't see why not. Thirty seconds later, I had it, Francis J. Crosby, 2134 Lantern Lane, St. Louis, Missouri. I thanked her profusely and got off the phone. I had a few more pieces to put together and it was time to call Ben.

An hour later, I telephoned Ben and told him that I had his father's location. He asked me where my office was located, which was about twenty-five minutes from where he lived. I swear he was there in fifteen minutes.

Without disclosing my source, I informed Ben that his biological father now resided in St. Louis and was president of a private company with forty employees. The company performed contract work for the military. I had his home and work numbers. "What do you want to do, Ben?"

A day Ben had longed for nearly all his life had arrived and he was coming out of his skin with excitement. A degree of hesitation and fear tempered the natural high. I knew exactly where he was. What if this guy wanted nothing to do with him? What if he denied anything to do with his conception? There were a lot of "what ifs" and only one way to answer them.

"Do you want to call him or do you want me to do it for you?"

Yielding to experience blended with no emotional attachment to the situation, Ben asked me to make the call.

I had made this type of call many times and even with no direct emotional attachment to the situation, you would have to be an ice cube not to feel the profound scope of the moment. With Ben sitting across from me, I placed the call. It was easy to get by the first screen, the company receptionist who connected me to Mr. Crosby's office, which resulted in his assistant playing defense.

"May I ask who is calling, please?"

"Yes, certainly, my name is Dave Smaha."

"And this is in reference to what, Mr. Smaha?"

I loved this part. "Well, it's rather confidential, I'm a state licensed private investigator, and I have an extremely important piece of information to convey to him. I sincerely believe he will want to take my call."

"Hold on, please," which meant he was there and it was just a matter of time before—

"This is Frank Crosby, how can I help you?"

"Mr. Crosby, thank you for taking my call. My name is Dave Smaha. I'm a state-licensed private investigator and I need to speak with you for a minute (without a pause, I continued). Although I always prefer doing this in person, face-to-face, the distance between us precludes that."

By now, I've got to believe that he's thinking, get on with it. I know I have his undivided attention.

"Mr. Crosby, I was hired to locate you by a young man who has just learned from his mother that you are his biological father. He is a wonderful guy who hopes that he can meet you." Normally around this time, my slow steady dialogue gets interrupted with the receiver of the call wanting to dictate the direction of the situation and this was no exception to that pattern.

Frank blurted out, "Oh dear God, I've wondered if this day would ever come. I think about him every day of my life. How is he? Where is he?"

Perfect, I thought, he's OK with it, which is not always the way it went. In the past, I had been threatened or met with complete denial. It was not uncommon to have the guy call the mother a slut and add, "You better keep looking because she screwed everybody." There was often an immediate reference to money or pleading poverty. That was not the case with Frank Crosby.

After answering some questions easing his concern for any bitterness felt by Ben, Frank asked me how he could speak to his son. With a sense of great pride and feeling every bit of the emotion of the uniting, I told Frank that it would not be difficult because Ben was sitting in my office.

"The next voice you hear, Frank, is your son, Ben. God bless."

I placed my hand tightly over the phone and whispered to Ben, "He is so happy to hear from you, relish this moment. I'm going to step out for a coffee. Take all the time you need. Good luck, man!"

The situation was tough enough for this great kid. I didn't want to provide any additional burden by being there and making him self-conscious. Based on prior experience, this type of call can get pretty emotional.

When I returned fifteen minutes later, I could hear that he was still talking, so I remained in the hall until he was finished. A few minutes later, there was silence.

I was greeted with a big hug from a physically fit young man who just wanted to let out some pure joy. Ben told me that it was his dream coming true. His father didn't want any more time to pass without them knowing each other. They talked about having a lot of time to make up and that they were both committed to trying to do that. Frank was Fed-Exing round trip first class airplane tickets the next day and Ben was going to St. Louis!

Through all the excitement, Ben took out his checkbook and started to write a check.

"Hold on, I'll make a deal with you. Instead of four hundred, make it two hundred with one condition. You gotta call me and let me know how it goes. I really want to know."

Ben departed but left behind a warm feeling in my heart. I couldn't love my job any more than I did at that moment.

Four days later, I got a phone call from Ben. The reception wasn't clear, as there was considerable background noise.

"Dave, it's Ben, can you hear me?"

"Hey, Ben, yeah, how's it going?"

"Dave, it's so good. I'm sitting with my father in the front row at Busch Stadium at the Cardinals opening day baseball game. Did you hear that, Dave? I'm at a baseball game with my dad. I never thought I'd say those words."

And then fighting a rage of pure emotion and having waited so long to be able to say those words, he said it again. "I'm at a baseball game with my dad!"

After being thanked profusely, we agreed to get together for a beer when he got home. I would later get an invitation to and attend his wedding where I was able to meet his father.

I realized at that moment how I had taken for granted growing up going to Fenway Park every year with my dad to watch our beloved visiting New York Yankees and then occasionally taking a road trip to New York City and visiting the House That Ruth Built, Yankee Stadium.

* * *

CHAPTER 2

WHERE THE GIRLS ARE

I have conducted many insurance investigations. Of the literally thousands, a few stand out as being unique and amusing.

As part of the standard insurance claim process, the claimant is often required to respond to interrogatories, which is fancy legal jargon for saying written questions. A claimant also may be deposed. This is where an individual is sworn to tell the truth under oath and required to respond to questioning similar to testifying, all done outside of the courtroom setting, but in a legal arena with a court reporter.

Between the interrogatories and the deposition, a claimant often gets locked into a position that will serve as a catalyst to my involvement. Many legitimate injuries are jeopardized with the loss of credibility based upon a claimant's assertion that he or she is physically unable to do certain activities or has not been gainfully employed while suffering from his or her injuries.

Proving either that a claimant can perform certain physical behavior he or she claims not to be capable of or showing that he or she is making money under the table, which is a violation of the process, is a profound victory for the insurance company. Naturally, finding someone engaged in both is a home run!

* * *

It was a Friday evening and I had just blown off my friends, who wanted to go out to have a few drinks at happy hour. I told them I had a case to work on and I would catch up with them later. "What is it, not another massage parlor? Are you really meeting us or just using the 'I have a case' excuse?" Granted, my job did afford me the wonderful opportunity to be excused from just about anything, anytime, anywhere. This time it was real. I was off to the American Legion Hall in a nearby town and I was running a few minutes late.

The parking lot was full. A quick drive through the lot revealed the claimant's vehicle. I was working on a tip and so far, so good. I parked my car and made my way to the main entrance, a pair of large solid metal doors. As I opened the door, it made a loud squeaking noise and then crashed closed behind me. There I stood, facing over a hundred little old ladies seated at rows of tables. Every single one of them noted my entrance as they all turned to see this young man who was obviously lost. It was beano night!

I quickly assessed the room and made my way to the left where two women were seated behind a smaller check-in table. I could hear the level of chatter rise behind me; the number caller used his microphone to ask for quiet before announcing the next number, "B-24."

At the reception table, I smiled at the women and immediately professed my lack of knowledge for the game. "Good evening, I need your help. I have never played beano before, but I have a first date next week with a really nice girl I met in church who plays all the time. She asked me to accompany her, which I want to do. I thought I'd try to play before my date with her so I don't look stupid." Well they bought it hook, line, and sinker, and before I knew it, I was walking toward a table that had some room remaining carrying four beano cards.

As I made my way across the room, the players were consumed with the game in process. The numbers were called out every few seconds and the room was hushed. This was a serious game. I took my seat and placed my four cards in front of me for the next game. I inconspicuously looked around the room trying not to attract too much attention. I couldn't help but think, *If my friends could see me now*, especially because it was Friday night, a night I had ordained as "boys' night."

I was amazed as I observed some of these women playing dozens of cards simultaneously. As a number was called, they went into action with two hands flying across the card-covered table in front of them. Then, when a game ended and the winner was confirmed, out came the magnetic wand and with a few fluid strokes, the chips were gathered—ready for the next game. To think, that this went on every Friday evening while I was out with my buddies on boys' night.

In between games, I drew the attention of some of my tablemates. Feeling like my alibi was extremely well received at the entrance, I redelivered it and hit another home run. I could see the story being passed along down the row of white-haired little old ladies. These women were loving and embracing their new player. Throughout the next few games, a random older lady would walk by me and ask, "How are you doing, dear?" or "Before you know it, you'll be playing fifty-four cards like Norma Jeanne, the beano queen!" Bingo! Well, not really but Norma Jeanne, the beano queen, as she was known in these parts, was my girl, the claimant in an insurance matter, and tonight, the subject of my investigation.

Norma was out of work with a bilateral carpal tunnel injury and had recently been deposed. During her deposition, she talked about how limiting her work-related injury was on her day-to-day activities. Besides not being able to perform normal day-to-day activity, she also claimed not to be able to play beano. She stated under oath that her painful limitation prevented her from playing a game she had enjoyed for thirty years. My job, which I chose to accept, was to find her playing beano, provide a detailed description of her movement and motion, and if possible, document her activity with photos or better yet, video. This was a matter of credibility, and to catch her in a lie, under oath, was a damaging blow to the value of her claim.

During the fifteen-minute intermission, I found Norma Jeanne drinking coffee and conversing with a few other ladies. I had been provided with a photograph by her employer and was certain I had the right gal, despite the fact that—I swear—every woman in the room had her hair done by the same hairdresser. As the game resumed, I followed Norma with my eyes and was able to wiggle myself into a position affording me a clear view of her playing area. It was a few minutes after 8:00 p.m. and I had determined through conversations that the night ended around 9:00.

At first, I thought to myself that maybe Norma Jeanne had bad body odor because she sat with a large gap between her and the next players at her table. Upon further scrutiny, the three- or four-foot gap was to accommodate the sea of beano cards in front of her covering a wide span of tabletop. With each number called, she went into fast furious action using both hands to cover the numbers on her cards.

That evening, with the use of a tiny hidden camera, I was able to obtain a dozen clear photographs of Norma Jeanne in action. I also carefully observed her in order to accurately describe her activity in a report I would dictate upon leaving the beano hall. Prior experience testifying in these matters had me noting things like the claimant exhibiting no signs of pain or discomfort in her movements and that she wore no brace or support device of any kind.

An hour later, I was in a bar with my friends. I could not stop thinking about the "beano queen." Man, if only she was forty years younger!

I felt a little bad Monday morning as I verbally reported my findings to the insurance adjuster. She didn't feel bad at all. In fact, by the sound of her voice, I had just made her day, week, and maybe longer. A few hours later, I received a telephone call from the attorney handling this claim.

Anticipating a showdown, the attorney wanted to make his case as secure and foolproof as possible. There was always the potential of Norma Jeanne testifying that the night I caught her playing beano was a one-time thing. She could say that she missed this aspect of her social life so much that she decided to give it a try. We had heard it before. Despite the agony it caused during and after her playing, she was desperate to attempt to play the game she so dearly missed. I had actually seen this approach work to gain the sympathy of the deciding party in a case. The injured worker was so devastated that he endured the agony for a taste of the life he had been victimized to abandon.

To be prepared to counterpunch that angle, I was requested to revisit Friday night beano and document Norma Jeanne one more time in consecutive weeks.

I had somehow miraculously been able to penetrate the beano world once but going back, as they say, could be difficult. I pulled out the girlfriend card I had already laid the groundwork for and kept my fingers crossed. The thought of being made in a hall of a hundred hostile white-haired beano players was one of the more frightening scenarios I had envisioned in a good long time as a private investigator.

A little before 7:00 p.m. we arrived at the Legion Hall. It had been a rough afternoon taking the wrath of the Friday night boys' night contingent as I tried to explain the rigors and demands of my chosen profession. Incorporating my girlfriend, Renee, into the equation was raising serious doubts and concern among the guys. They had a difficult time believing that I would miss boys' night two weeks in a row...and this week I was working the case with my girlfriend!

I was almost a little disappointed when I observed Norma Jeanne's vehicle in the lot. The value of her claim was about to be greatly reduced, despite the fact that she likely had legitimate pain, discomfort, and limited work capacity. Her love and passion for her game was jeopardizing her decisions. I could see the entire matter playing out in my head. She likely wasn't even honest with her own attorney, who might even turn on her as I testified to my findings.

Upon entering the hall shortly before the start time, I was greeted by several of my old (literally) friends who were "just delighted" to see me again. And of course, they noticed on my arm, my beautiful young date, the culmination of my alibi.

"And this must be the girl you told us about. What a lucky young man you are." The attention immediately shifted to Renee, who was the "beano player" of the two of us. The "cuteness" of the situation earned me a few accolades, but I couldn't help but think that had my alibi been the truth, these old bitches were throwing me under the bus by telling Renee how I had been there last week learning the game all because they thought it was "so sweet."

With the assistance of my lovely and distracting partner combined with the fact that when the game was on, these women were focused, I was able to click off a dozen additional photos. I also captured Norma Jeanne in all her glory using a miniature digital video camera. Although the photos would confirm her playing the game, they could not do justice to her action as provided with the video.

As we departed the hall that evening, I couldn't help but wonder if the group would ever be made aware of my deceptive practice in the beano hall. Renee and I were invited back no fewer than ten times, although I realized that might not be safe. Within days, my findings would likely threaten the claimant and her lawyer. My work here was complete.

For the record, I never won a single game of beano but Norma Jeanne won three times during the two nights I played.

As is often the case, the matter was settled out of the legal arena with Norma Jeanne getting a greatly reduced lump sum settlement and likely never admitting to anyone that she had been investigated.

* * *

CHAPTER 3

WHEN IN ROME

Harry Littlefield, a fifty-nine-year-old man, worked as a transfer driver for a high-end courier company. After a minor car accident while at work, Harry, his attorney, and his doctor all claimed he could no longer drive and therefore was entitled to continued ongoing workers' compensation benefits. Harry was a retired navy veteran who had taken early retirement in his early fifties and had worked as a driver for the past six years until the accident. The medical findings revealed a soft tissue injury, a relatively subjective diagnosis, making capacity and range of motion a very difficult thing to substantiate or prove.

The compensation Harry was entitled to receive was calculated at the rate of two-thirds of his previous years' average weekly wage. The payments were tax-free, so Harry was taking home very close to what he took home while working. In light of the fact that Harry's wife was now retired and the couple loved to travel, there was not much incentive for Harry to return to his daily work.

Although the competing medical opinions differed on the extent of the effects of the injury, one thing on which they did concur was that Harry was at or near his recuperation end result. It was time for this case to be heard, and a disposition to be reached.

Harry had responded to interrogatories and had been deposed. In each case, under oath, he had made the claim that his pain, discomfort, and limited range of motion made driving extremely difficult, caused immeasurable pain, and made him feel endangered. I can tell you from experience that Harry did not think up those words. He had carefully rehearsed them at the coaching of his attorney, who stood to personally gain with a higher settlement.

Harry also alleged that his recently retired wife carried the burden of his inability to drive. With another careful selection of words, Harry conceded that on a few occasions, he had attempted to drive, "hoping and praying" that he could resume a normal lifestyle. After each attempt, he realized that driving was an activity he was not capable of enduring. Harry acknowledged under cross-examination that in the case of an emergency, he believed that he would attempt to operate a vehicle in a very precautionary manner.

The insurance company and its legal counsel viewed this documented response as a premeditated alibi, an affirmative defense, in case anyone investigated Harry and caught him behind the wheel. In so many cases, claimants would exaggerate their limitations only to be caught and lose credibility, which nearly always resulted in serious damage to the value of the claim. In Harry's matter, a heavyweight in the personal injury legal arena represented him. This attorney coached his clients well and they rarely cornered themselves with restrictive claims. After all, it did not mean that Harry could work just because he drove to the local store every now and then, especially when put in the context of his "attempt to want to lead a normal life."

With the case rapidly approaching the medical result and a final hearing imminent, I was retained to conduct surveillance on Mr. Littlefield. An insurance company loss would equate to six figures of future payments and/or a lump sum settlement.

"Let's see what Harry does when he doesn't think anyone is watching" was how the insurance company adjuster conveyed her request. As I reviewed the case before conducting surveillance, I couldn't help but notice the coincidental timing of Harry's wife retiring and Harry's "inability" to return to work.

Preliminary work revealed two vehicles registered to Harry and Delores Littlefield, a late-model Buick sedan and a three-year-old Ford pickup truck—in and of itself, meaningless, yet certainly enough to warrant a closer look.

I located the Littlefield residence early on a Tuesday morning in mid-November. Both vehicles were parked in the driveway, which ran along the side of an old but very well-kept Colonial-style residence. I could find no inconspicuous vantage point from which a stationary surveillance could be maintained. The house was situated on a somewhat rural road with major intersections and highways approximately a mile in either direction. It was very difficult to determine which direction one would take upon departing the driveway. It was a coin flip, so I maintained stationary surveillance east of the residence combining periodic drive-bys to see if I had guessed wrong.

Sure enough, just after 8:00 a.m., a drive by the residence revealed the Buick no longer present. I had a fifty-fifty chance as to which direction they might take and my luck was not good. How soon that luck would change.

I called my friend Angela at the local newspaper. I was going to have her place a courtesy call to see how the Littlefields' newspaper delivery service had been. The real reason was to determine whether anyone was at home. If Harry and Delores had departed, I was done for now on this case and I would resume another day. However, if an older gentleman answered, I could stay put and keep an eye open for the pickup truck to move.

Although I could have made a call using the pretext of a wrong number, I had to factor in two conditions. First, the case was nearing finality and second, Harry was represented by a very savvy attorney who had undoubtedly warned him to be cautious of anything suspicious, whatsoever, including anonymous calls, frequent drive-bys, and who knows what else. I didn't want to spook Harry.

As Angela pulled up the account on her computer, she told me that I owed her "big time." Harry and Delores Littlefield had called the previous week to suspend newspaper delivery as of Wednesday, November 17, stating the reason as traveling to Florida. That was tomorrow!

All sorts of question arose with the most relative being, would they drive, and if so, who would drive? I called my good friend and fellow private investigator, Kevin Donnelly, and told him I needed him for the following morning. Without hesitating or even knowing why, Kevin responded, "You got it. Where and what time?"

The next morning at 5:00 a.m., Kevin was positioned at a post east of the residence. I was situated up the road west of the Littlefield home. Both vehicles were in the driveway and there were lights on within the residence.

Equipped with two-way radios, Kevin and I kept each other amused with our radio banter. At 6:15 a.m., a drive-by revealed the trunk of the Buick open and a man fitting the description of Harry Littlefield hoisting a large suitcase into the trunk.

"Stand by Kevin; it's almost time to fly south!" Situations like these never failed to get the adrenaline flowing. The last thing you wanted to do at this critical juncture was blow it either by losing them or getting made.

We patiently waited and then BAM! Kevin blurted into his radio, "I've got 'em coming at me, and I'm on them."

"Stick tight," I responded, "I'm on my way, and we'll rotate."

"Dave, he's fucking driving!"

"DON'T LOSE 'EM."

Within a minute, I was relieving Kevin and had taken the first position in tailing the Buick. After a trip to the Dunkin' Donut drive-through, the car proceeded directly onto Interstate 95 South.

We spent the next eight and a half hours carefully following Harry Littlefield, who drove the entire day, despite being accompanied in the car by his wife. Dozens of photos were taken, some strategically timed to incorporate Harry driving as he passed signs welcoming him to Massachusetts and Connecticut and New Jersey. We also video-taped him when we drove diagonally behind him in his left rear blind spot.

Further photos were taken as the Littlefields stopped for lunch, at which point we ditched Kevin's vehicle in a twenty-four-hour supermarket parking lot. At that stage, there was no suspicion and we could relax in our tailing activity.

One of the most useful signs that most people take for granted are the ones that tell you how many miles until the next exit. If you know that there are ten miles until the next exit and you get a good indication of the speed someone averages, it is very easy to lie back completely out of view and then close the gap as an exit approaches. Once they pass the exit, you do it again, and again and again. Of course, tollbooths are the worst enemies—the fear of getting behind the stupid fucking idiot who tosses his change into the bucket and either misses or remains idle because the green light didn't come on.

I've actually seen someone get out of a vehicle to look for the coin that missed its mark, not find it, and then walk to another booth with a dollar bill in hand looking for change. The lesson you learn through the years is never to get pinned in by someone behind you. Leave enough space, whether at a tollbooth or a traffic light so that you can proceed forward and take another route.

This surveillance was seamless. After nearly nine hours of Harry driving, the Buick turned off at the Atlantic City, New Jersey, exit and eventually parked at a nice motel across from the main strip of high-rise casinos. One last photograph was taken as Harry emerged from the car. At that point, we thought our day was done. Little did we know, our adventure was about to begin.

Feeling 100 percent confident that our subject had no idea, whatsoever, that we had been with him all day, I followed him into the lobby and got a real good look at him for identification purposes, which I anticipated down the road. It was always a plus when the claimant had a tattoo when it came time to positively identify someone. Harry had a tattoo of an eagle and the American flag on his left forearm. In the back of many investigators' minds were the identification horror stories that were told through the years in our circle. After believing you had nailed a case, you get hit with a "that wasn't me" defense. On one occasion, one of my colleagues went through all the motions of documenting and testifying about his observations of a claimant to be hit with the testimony that the claimant had an identical twin brother who would testify that it was he who had been followed and videotaped…ouch! For many reasons, many of which were created and designed by knowledge-able, crafty, and completely dishonest and greedy attorneys, you could never get enough nails in the coffin.

After getting a second-floor room just above where the Littlefields' Buick was parked, Kevin and I settled in and prepared for a rapid departure should that be necessary. There was always the chance that our snowbirds would get up very early for a full day of travel. We were positioned so that by keeping our room window open, we could clearly hear the starting of a car from our second-floor perch. I figured that we could be out of the room with our stuff and into our car in less than a minute in addition to having viewed the direction the Buick departed. It was a pretty safe assumption they would head for the highway going south.

I believe that conducting surveillance and following people can be addictive. Not that we hadn't had a completely successful day, but when Harry and Delores set out on foot, Kevin and I were safely, carefully, and inconspicuously behind them. It was game; it was sport; and you never knew what you might learn!

After a casual quick dinner at the high-rise casino/hotel across the street from their room, Delores headed back alone as Harry strolled into the casino. Kevin made sure she made it back safely as I stayed on my boy. Ten minutes later, Kevin returned and we watched Harry scouting out blackjack tables. He found one he liked—maybe because the dealer was a gorgeous tall blond who looked as if she stepped out of the pages of *Playboy*. Harry bought some chips and began playing.

Although in the back of my mind I believed I could be making a mistake being viewed by Harry, I could not resist taking a seat at the same table as soon as one opened up. As players sometimes do, we started a little light and casual conversation, as we were all in this together and playing against this statuesque beauty. Fortunately, the dealer was on a roll of breaking, and paid out eight of my first ten hands, putting the group in a jovial mood.

As the dealer, Julie reshuffled and cashed a couple of players out, I engaged a few players in a "where you from" kind of conversation. Within minutes, Harry was chatting and offering that he was from Maine and en route to Florida for the winter. Of significance was his offering that he and his wife were going to stay in Atlantic City for three days and then go to New York City for Thanksgiving. My visions of Daytona Beach quickly faded; however, my decision to sit at the table proved to be fruitful.

I was loving my job as I sat there winning a few hundred bucks, and actually rooting for Harry to win some money. He had no idea how bad a day he was having; no matter how much he won in black-jack, today he lost a lot of money.

Shortly before 8:00 p.m., Harry glanced at his watch, cashed out winnings of at least three hundred dollars and bolted as if he had some place to be. He sure did. Kevin followed him to the casino ballroom, which was advertising in bright lights on the marquee, TONIGHT!!! THE FINALS OF THE MISS NUDE NEW JERSEY PAGEANT...8:00 PM.

Not wanting to raise suspicion, I played a few more games, cashed out, and joined Kevin at the bar in the ballroom after coughing up the fifty-dollar admission fee. I wondered how that would look on my expense sheet! Harry was perched at a stand-up bar affording a nice view of the run-way. *Could this day get any more difficult,* I thought to myself. *Work, work, work!*

After securing a great position from which we could observe our friend, we settled in for a lit-tle entertainment. We watched and photographed Harry as he squandered his blackjack winnings on a couple of drinks and tips, but primarily on this hot and fiery redheaded waitress who was giving Harry her undivided attention.

In return, the buxom and topless waitress/ dancer seemed to be getting compensated handsomely by Harry as she danced, hugged, gyrated, and grinded her body against his. As we looked around the room, it was not uncommon. The guys were out for some nudity and sexuality and the girls were out to give them what they wanted and take their money. Easy come, easy go, Harry!

It was captivatingly amusing to watch the ladies (used in the loosest of contexts) work the guys. They seemed to have a knack at determining instantly who was going to fork it over and who was cheap and just wanted to have a free look and see. Harry was forking it over and Kevin was moving in with his low light video. He was getting it all—it was truly the sport of it, the game. Kevin had his game on as I relaxed at my post and thoroughly enjoyed the visual feast.

At 8:30 p.m., the crowd was getting a little restless for the show to begin. My thinking was that the owner had a packed house and was in no hurry to shorten his lucrative evening. I was wrong. The delay was a technical difficulty.

Two well-dressed men approached me and asked if they could speak with me for a moment.

"Sure, what's up?"—Sort of ready for nearly anything.

"You from around here?" one of the men asked in a not so casual way.

"No, just passing through, on business," I responded, trying to be vague until I knew where this was going.

Then the other guy pops the next question, "Do you know any of the contestants in the pageant?"

I thought about a clever response of *not yet*, but it wasn't that kind of conversation so I simply responded that I did not. Then it became clear what these men needed.

"It turns out that one of the twelve judges had a prior relationship with one of the girls in the contest and has had to be recused of his duties."

Pretty fancy talk for a goon, I'm thinking, as I kept my best poker face.

He continued, "We need to replace him, as contest rules dictate a scoring system using twelve judges. If you're interested, the pay isn't great, but if you are even close to normal, the benefits are better than health insurance."

Not wanting to appear overanxious, I exchanged a few questions and answers and within a minute, I was committed for the next two hours for a hundred bucks, a two-hundred-dollar bar credit and other benefits that had piqued my curiosity. As I followed the men to a room behind the stage, I recall thinking ever so briefly, *Where's Kevin?*

I was given some very brief training and a scorecard with the names of each contestant and the eight categories on which to rate them from one to ten. I was then led to a front and center table at which my fellow judges were seated. The judges sat in a sort of orchestra pit that was very private and very dimly lit. Before I had pulled in my chair and introduced myself to my neighbors at the table, the light show began and a tuxedo-clad host emerged onto the stage. The show would go on!

I sent Kevin a text message so he wouldn't worry. I had abandoned my work duties for the good of pageantry!

It didn't take long to figure out the benefit package. Besides the basic categories of Stage Presence, Appearance, Movement, and Style, there were things like Body Tone, Personality, and Sexuality—funny, no Swimsuit or Evening Gown!

After a girl pranced around the stage for a while, and as the next girl began, the contestant made her way to the judge's area. For one judge at a time, she worked her score by displaying her goods. It took me a girl or two and some coaching by the judges sitting next to me to realize my role. These girls wanted and expected the judges to feel them anywhere and everywhere. How else would we be able to rate their Body Tone or experience their Sexuality? The girls were not shy, as they took my hands and placed them where I may not otherwise go. It became extraordinarily apparent as to why the judge's pit was dark and private. The goons' reference to the benefits was also abundantly clear. I just kept wondering how I got myself into this.

In case you are wondering, after three rounds of elimination and with the final three contestants working their tails as well as other body parts, the judges came to a near unanimous decision that the hard-bodied Kathy Ireland look-alike was the winner. I don't know what she did in the pit, but when she emerged in the final round on her hands and knees and crawled across the stage with the most unbelievable bedroom eyes, she already had me. Of course, I couldn't let her know that as she shared her sixty seconds of one-on-one pit time with me! That just wouldn't be good judging!

After meeting up with Kevin and filling him in with my difficult evening, he told me what he had been up to. Apparently, Harry and his new red-haired friend had really hit it off and struck a deal that Kevin was able to overhear and witness. For a rate of ten dollars a minute, and a ten-minute minimum, she would take him to a private VIP room and entertain him "without all these people around," as she put it. Harry paid her $150 and out back they went for just over fifteen minutes. Easy come, easy go!

After a long day, we enjoyed a great night of sleep knowing our subject was not heading out the following day. After checking in with the insurance adjuster and attorney, we all felt we had enough on Harry.

I submitted a very detailed report, including all of Harry's activity. In this case, the report went to the opposing counsel with a demand to drop the claim or face insurance fraud charges, which could lead to criminal and civil judgment implications. In lieu of a promise not to pursue the matter, Harry dropped his claim.

I often wondered about the most valuable part of our investigative findings. Was it catching Harry driving for nine hours or Harry's fear that his wife would become aware of his casino adventure? I realized long ago that there were some things I would never know, yet at the same time have a good idea.

One of the "benefits" of this job was getting up close and personal with twelve very attractive females, not to mention being encouraged to assess overall body tone...first hand. I wasn't sure if I would ever have that opportunity again my entire life. It got me thinking and trying to compare these benefits with other perks I had received through the years.

You see, in the insurance investigative arena, if I determined that a claimant was engaged in some business activity, part of my work would be to hire those services in order to document the evidence. To prove that someone was earning money or gainfully employed was one degree of investigative finding, but add to that the claimant being physically active and the case was well built. Along those lines, and at the expense of insurance companies through the years, I have had my home professionally landscaped, a new roof installed, a new driveway put in, my chimney cleaned, my home cleaned as well as painted, hardwood floors sanded, plumbing work performed, and my electrical system updated and made to accept a generator. I rode in a limo, was massaged from head to toe, and even had the services of a personal trainer, but throughout it all, the most memorable, enjoyable, and beneficial benefit of them all had to be in the arts.

* * *

CHAPTER 4

BAD COP—BAD COP

The "color of the law" is a phrase often used in the criminal justice system. It is most often spewed by prosecutors attempting to enhance the credibility of testimony being offered by an individual in law enforcement. Enhancing credibility is often what verdicts boil down to when a fact or a statement is one person's word against another's. It is often said in the legal system that credibility is everything.

When a police officer, or the color of the law, testified about something, the typical juror believes it. They want to believe it. Now, take two officers, wearing the color of the law who both testify to a confession. Throw in some physical evidence linking the defendant with the crime weapon corroborated by an analyst from the state crime laboratory, a defendant with a slightly marred past, and chances are you got yourself a conviction.

* * *

It was July 4 and that meant one thing in Northshire, Maine…the Colton party. Every year for as far back as anyone could recall, celebrating our nation's independence was synonymous with the biggest bash these parts experienced. Everyone in town knew it. No invitations were necessary. It was tradition.

Despite the large number of people and the copious volume of alcohol consumed, the well-organized event planned for these factors and handled them with expertise developed over the years. Throngs of partygoers arrived with tents and pop-up campers. A few of the area's more affluent would arrive and showcase their RVs. At the crack of daylight, volunteers were on the premises directing early arrivals to the big open field adjacent to the barn and accommodating their setting up base camp. The barn, where the party peaked, was where the band played until the sun rose on a new day.

There was a status level that went along with being a volunteer. You earned that privilege to wear (and keep) the red, white, and blue T-shirt, which exuded authority and empowered that person to remove anyone perceived to be out of control or disruptive. In this particular year, there were over thirty certified volunteers.

The owners of the property and annual hosts, the Coltons, were a fifth- or sixth-generation local family consisting of the mother, Lisa, a thirty-six-year-old single mother, and three teenage children, two girls and the eldest, a boy. Her husband and the father of the children had been killed in Desert Storm five years earlier, leaving Lisa to raise the children by herself. The death of her husband only served to fuel the strong and patriotic dedication of the annual event.

Lisa worked hard at motherhood as well as holding down a full-time job working for the state labor department. She was very well liked by everyone and not just because she was extremely attractive and built like no one else for hundreds of miles around. Men and women alike were awed by her beauty and genuine kindness. After her husband died, Lisa did not date anyone for several years; then she dated only occasionally when workmates or friends tried to arrange for her happiness and companionship. The matchmaking never got beyond second dates. The closest thing to a relationship was with a man, Quinn, who lived nearby who was a good-looking, divorced, former friend of Lisa's deceased husband.

Quinn had become the closest to Lisa of any of the men who had tried. As her former husband's friend, they had grieved together and Quinn was often around the house offering his manly assistance. He repeatedly reminded Lisa that he had given Brian, her deceased husband, his word that if anything ever happened to him, he would be there to help her. Lisa's oldest, Brent, didn't like any part of Quinn, including his accurate perception that Quinn wanted a lot more than to help out. Brent had also witnessed, on many occasions, Quinn being drunk and obnoxious. He had also been the one to call the police nine months earlier when Quinn wouldn't leave one evening and became verbally and physically abusive to Lisa and her children.

A local police officer named Stanley Griffin arrived just in time and saved the day by getting Quinn out of there, and charging him with a variety of criminal offenses. Lisa agreed as the victim, to a combination of a restraining order and the condition that Quinn participate in an alcohol treatment program to include no use of alcohol. It had become a well-known fact that Quinn had a drinking problem and needed help.

For his part, Stanley took on the role as the knight in shining armor. He made no secret of his quest to win over Lisa Colton and professed to everyone at the Sunrise Breakfast Diner his intentions. It had almost taken on a fairy-tale feel, like when Gaston openly sought and predicted he would marry Belle in *Beauty and the Beast*. Sgt. Stanley Griffin often stopped by the house to check on their safety. Once again, eighteen-year-old Brent saw through it and made it crystal clear that he not only didn't respect Stanley's authority, but that he also hated his guts. Stanley had played a role in many previous altercations with local youth, including Brent and his friends. Brent claimed that Griffin was a corrupt cop who took the law into his own hands and handed out his own justice in the form of police brutality. No one could ever prove it, as Stanley knew how to carry out his activity while flying below the radar.

After failing to win over the beautiful Lisa, Stanley Griffin believed and professed that the only thing standing between him and Lisa Colton was Brent Colton.

The party that year was impeccable, aided by warm summer weather and a record crowd. Everyone was having a great time dancing in the moonlight, as the band was able to perform outside on a makeshift stage near the barn. Many were still marveling at what was being heralded as the biggest fireworks display ever! Even Quinn, the estranged neighbor, showed up and was allowed to remain after being warned by Lisa to be on his best behavior or risk being banned for life.

No one would ever agree as to exactly how it got started; however, shortly after 1:00 a.m., a major brawl broke out in the main house. Although the hope was always not to involve the police, who waited anxiously nearby looking for a reason to break up the event they naturally were opposed to, in this case, it was deemed necessary.

When the blinking blue lights came speeding up the long driveway, self-preservation dictated and most dispersed. Sergeant Griffin was the first police officer to arrive on the scene and would later provide a detailed report of what he observed.

Quinn was lying motionless on the kitchen floor in a pool of blood and bleeding heavily from an open gash to the neck area. Brent Colton was on his knees next to him with knife, with an approximately ten-inch blade, in his hands. Colton, who was highly intoxicated, dropped the knife upon the arrival of the police.

Quinn had lost a lot of blood and was believed near dead. Emergency personnel got him out of there and rushed him to the hospital. Lisa Colton was visibly upset and very loud in her attempt to clarify the situation. With everyone yelling at once, the scene was chaotic. The police secured the scene by removing anyone who tried to stay around out of curiosity. Brent, who had sustained some heavy blows in the melee, was bloodied and having a difficult time being coherent. Sergeant Griffin removed him by guiding him by the arm out the door leading to his cruiser. He did so at the objection of Lisa, who continued to verbally abuse Sergeant Griffin. The knife was placed into an evidence bag and numerous blood samples were taken. The party was over!

In years past, the days following the big bash were filled with stories of good times and recollection. This year was quite different. The rumor mill was raging. Brent Colton had been charged with attempted murder. As Quinn remained in intensive care clinging to life, the locals with firsthand experience with the criminal justice system held court at the local diners and coffee shops. Eighteen-year-old Brent would be tried as an adult and was facing up to twenty years...and that was if he was lucky and Quinn survived. If he died, then the charge would be upgraded to murder and that's twenty-five to life!

The evidence was mounting and none of it was good. The knife secured at the scene was processed through the state crime lab. It not only had Brent's fingerprints on it, the blade was covered with Quinn's blood. Sergeant Griffin, well aware of the players, obtained statements from four individuals claiming to have heard Brent express his hatred toward Quinn and even a couple of repeated threats they claim he made about wanting to "kill that bastard." However, tipping the scale and most damaging of all was the confession received by Sergeant Griffin and his colleague, Officer Woods, in which Brent acknowledged his attempt to kill Quinn.

After turning the scene over to the evidence technicians, Griffin and Woods visited the hospital. Quinn was unconscious and on life-sustaining equipment. Brent Colton, who had been transported to the hospital to treat various cuts that needed stitches, was admitted for observation in lieu of being sent to the county jail. Griffin and Hardy interviewed him and subsequently detailed his confession in the police report. Brent acknowledged a long-standing hatred toward the victim and admitted to trying to kill him in the early morning hours of July 5.

My investigation into the matter did not get off to any roaring start on behalf of the defense for Brent Colton. Nobody really wanted to get involved or go against the color of the law in fear of retribution. Brent wasn't much help for his part, claiming only that he didn't do it and that he didn't confess to anything. To top it all off and destroy his claims, he admitted to being highly intoxicated and not remembering much at all. The only thing working for Brent was that Quinn recovered from his life-threatening wound, thus keeping the charge reduced to the "attempted" version of murder.

To add fuel to the raging fire, Sergeant Griffin appeared on Lisa Colton's doorstep one evening and asked her if she would like to reconsider her refusal to date him, alluding to the fact that he may be able to help Brent's predicament. Of course, she spewed some vulgarity toward him. He subsequently would deny the incident ever took place.

With the case at number five on the docket list and at least two cases on the list above it working toward plea agreements, our time was running very thin. I had one last stone to turn over, and knew it was a long shot.

Likely, the most damaging hurdle Brent was facing was his confession. Juries had a difficult time believing that someone would admit to something they didn't do, and retracting a confession was always a formidable hurdle.

I visited the hospital where Brent was treated and was directed to the fifth floor. *Maybe there was a roommate or a nurse nearby,* I thought; *maybe he wasn't read his rights or maybe I could get lucky and find something I couldn't even fathom.*

I determined who was on duty during the morning in question by speaking to a nursing supervisor. It had been over four months since the day in question yet a couple of nurses I spoke with remembered the morning. They also remembered the police going into the room and closing the large wooden door behind them. They recalled and then confirmed by looking at records that although the room where Brent stayed was a double, no one else was in the room that day. I asked if I could see the room. After a few of the nurses looked at each other without appearing to be opposed, one of them said, "I don't see why not." As I always did, I expressed my sincere appreciation for their assistance and apologized for being an inconvenience.

The room was vacant, so I had the opportunity to check it out carefully. The nurse advised me that Brent had been in the bed farthest in and closest to the window. Being away from the crowded nurses' station, I sneaked a question in with my nurse escort. "Do you remember Brent?" I asked. "Very well," she replied.

I hesitated and said, "He's a pretty nice kid, and he is in a heap of trouble. What do you remember about Brent?"

The nurse cautiously told me that Brent was pretty banged up and very fired up upon admission to the hospital. In order to treat him, he was given some strong sedatives, keeping in mind it would be mixing with the alcohol he had obviously consumed. For the very first time, I was seeing a glimmer of hope.

"Was that medicated state induced before the cops got here?" That did it. She started to clam up, obviously sensing that I was intensifying my line of inquiry. My enthusiasm had not been contained. I had come on too strong and spooked her. It was extremely rare to get medical personnel to even talk to you, never mind spill their guts on sensitive matters within the first few minutes. I had screwed up and I knew it.

I had one last thing to do before I departed the hospital. It was my impassioned plea with the nurses hanging out at the station as my audience.

"I know it was four months ago and I know there are very strict guidelines about confidentiality—I truly respect that. I also know that you nurses are in the business of saving people's lives, and right now, I'm trying to save one too. There's a decent eighteen-year-old kid who is scared to death right now. He is looking at spending up to twenty years in jail for something he claims, and I believe, he did not do and never confessed to doing. I, for one, believe him but that's not enough. If someone knows anything that could help, please consider doing the right thing. There's a mother and two little sisters that would be forever grateful. I'm going to leave some of my cards. I don't care what time of day it is; if you know anything, please give me a call. We don't have much time. Thanks and good night."

Two weeks later, the trial began with opening statements by the prosecutor and defense attorney. The prosecutor told the jury that he was going to make their job easy. He paced in front of the jury box and dramatically proclaimed that the physical evidence in this case is straightforward and conclusive. Then he made his way over to the table at which Brent Colton was seated and raised his voice a notch. "And the defendant," pointing at Brent, "confessed to, not one but two, police officers that in the early morning hours of July 5, he tried to kill Quinn Charlton. You will hear from those police officers, and when you have heard the credible testimony and seen the irrefutable physical evidence, you will have no doubt in your mind that the verdict is guilty as charged. Thank you for your attentiveness."

The prosecutor then returned to his seat. It was the defense attorney's turn, and everybody in the room knew it. Rob sat for a moment pensively. I had worked with this attorney on dozens of cases and always admired his ability to adapt. He had an inherent quality to know exactly how to handle a situation. I had seen him act like an Al Pacino character and get remanded by a judge in open court. On other occasions, he would be quiet, and even hard to hear, resulting in jurors leaning over to get closer. Then at some critical moment in the trial, he would get extremely loud and exude anger and disgust, exactly what he would want the jury to feel at that moment. I didn't always, however, now I consider him a master. I always enjoyed working with him, never quite knowing how he was going to play his cards, which were often the findings of my investigative work on the matter.

On this date, he knew the prosecutor was confident. The jury was ready for his response to a very convincing and seemingly hard-to-beat opening statement. He wasn't going to try to win this one in the first inning. At the same time, he had to address the strength of his opponent. He paused and slowly stood at his table.

"Maybe we should all go home right now. Let's throw him in jail...next!" As he slowly made his way from behind the table to a podium, he continued. "But that's not how our system works, ladies and gentlemen. With all due respect to Mr. Prosecutor, he believes that he has this case all figured out. He is wrong...very, very wrong. You see, the problem is he doesn't have all the facts. He has one side of the story. Maybe he forgot his role, a lot like other people you will hear from. He (pointing to the prosecutor) is not the judge. He is (extending his hand toward the bench). The judge makes the rules, not the prosecutor. And he is not the jury, you are. What he thinks is not relevant. It does not matter one bit. You, the jury, will decide this case after hearing ALL the evidence, something no one has yet heard. And while it may seem like we (motioning between him and the prosecutor), disagree on many things, I agree with one thing he said. When you have heard all the evidence, your job will be easy. Thank you."

The trial got off to a typical boring start with crime scene technicians describing the scene. Rob had requested and was granted the sequestering of witnesses. This meant that anyone who could testify, with the exception of the defendant and a lead detective, had to remain out of the court-room while others testified. It also meant that any-one who had been in the courtroom could not speak to sequestered witnesses. This was done to ensure the integrity of testimony. It was common and it made perfect sense not to want witnesses swayed by testimony they heard prior to their tes-timony. Blood was examined at the lab and it was testified to that the knife had undoubtedly been in Brent Colton's hand. Rob would occasionally cross-examine a state witness more for clarification purposes than anything. He knew where his battle would be fought and it was as if he was saving his energy. Witness after witness, Rob would half stand and say, "I have no questions of this witness," and then resume his seated position.

The heat was turned up with the crime lab technician who was testifying just before a presumed lunch break. It was always important to leave off before a break or the end of the day with a strong piece. You wanted that evidence or testimony to resonate all through the break or overnight, whatever the case might be. And if it was important to the prosecution, it was just as important to the defense to attempt to combat that piece of evidence or testimony. Such was the case as this state witness testified that the neck laceration sustained by Quinn Charlton was consistent with the type of cut that the knife apprehended at the scene, and which had Brent Colton's fingerprints on it, would administer.

Unlike previous witnesses, Rob stood quickly when it was his time to cross-examine this witness. His blatant different and more aggressive behavior seemed to capture the attention of everyone in the courtroom.

"Mr. Horowitz, did you see the laceration on Quinn Charlton the night of the incident?"

"No, sir."

"Did you see Mr. Charlton's neck after it was stitched?"

"No, sir."

"Mr. Horowitz, have you ever in your entire life seen Quinn Charlton?"

"No, sir"

"Mr. Horowitz, do you know who the lead detective is in this matter?"

"Yes, Sergeant Griffin."

"Sergeant Stanley Griffin, correct?"

"Yes."

"And do you see Sergeant Stanley Griffin in the courtroom today?"

"Yes, I do, right there."

"Let the record show that the witness has pointed to Sergeant Stanley Griffin seated at the prosecutor's table. Mr. Horowitz, if you never saw Quinn Charlton, would you kindly tell us what you used to base your finding that the knife was consistent with the laceration to this individual you have never seen?"

"Yes, sir. The laceration was described in the medical report as likely being caused by a very sharp and pointed instrument. The report goes on to describe the laceration as being made by an instrument that had a thickness of approximately a quarter inch. That would rule out a razor blade or steak knife-like object. My testimony is that the knife is consistent with the medical analysis."

When the technician finished his little dissertation, he sat back almost cockily as if to say, "Take that." Rob snapped back immediately in order not to allow him to bask.

"How did the knife get to the lab, Mr. Horowitz?"

"Sergeant Griffin delivered it to the lab, sir"

"And how about the medical report…how did that get to you?"

"Same way," spoken with a tone exuding *where you going with this?*

"Mr. Horowitz, is this the medical report which you used to base your conclusion that the wound could have been administered by the knife in question?" As he waved the medical report exhibit previously admitted into evidence, before the jury, he approached the witness and handed it to him.

Mr. Horowitz looked briefly at the two-page document and nodded as he answered, "Yes."

"That is a copy, is it not, Mr. Horowitz?"

"Yes, it is."

"Mr. Horowitz, during any time of your analysis, did you ever see the original of this report?"

"No, but—"

"Mr. Horowitz, you've already answered the question, but I have a few more. Calling your attention to the bottom of the second page of the report, do you see two signatures?"

"Yes, I do."

"And would you read those names, please?"

"Yes, Sergeant Stanley Griffin and Officer Peter Woods."

"Mr. Horowitz, are those signatures notarized?"

"No, sir."

"Mr. Horowitz (with a raised volume and the tone exuding a little courtroom drama), did you see the individuals whose names appear on that report actually sign their names?"

"No, sir," with a tone of *aren't we grasping now?*

"So, it is possible that the signature of Peter Woods was signed by someone else, is it not?"

"I suppose that is possible—"

Interrupting the appearance that Horowitz was going to try to explain, Rob bellowed out, "That is all I have for this witness. Thank you, Your Honor."

After a few gyrations of testimony back and forth, it was determined that the original report was at the police station and that it was typical to use copies of police reports in the examination of evidence. It wasn't a home run; in fact, it wasn't even a base hit, in my opinion. At the most, it was a ball, but it was something. It was like planting a seed with the jury and at the same time, serving up a smokescreen to the prosecutor. You could see in his directives that the district attorney was going to get someone to produce the original report and then get Officer Woods into the courtroom to testify and dramatically clear the air of any doubt or suspicion surrounding the report and the authenticity of the signature.

After a lunch break, the trial resumed with the state's star witness, Sgt. Stanley Griffin. In full uniform attire, wearing the color of the law, Griffin gave detailed testimony of his arrival at the scene and then concluded by detailing his interview with Brent Colton at the hospital. Griffin stated that upon questioning, Colton told him that he wanted to and tried to kill Quinn Charlton with his knife. Griffin was provided his copy of the report; he proceeded to read off a handful of severely incriminating quotes proclaimed by Colton that night.

Just to nail the coffin, he added on a couple of occasions that during the confession, his partner, Officer Peter Woods, accompanied him. A glance at the jury suggested that they were buying it.

Then, almost as if he had nearly forgotten such a meaningless detail, the prosecutor said, "Oh, and one more thing, Sergeant Griffin, is that your signature on the bottom of page two of the police report?"

"Yes, sir, it certainly is," responded a cocky Sgt. Stanley Griffin.

The state confidently rested their case.

It was time for the defense to begin, but before they did, the attorneys had a brief discussion at the sidebar out of earshot of everyone. Rob dejectedly stated that he didn't have a very long defense and that he could likely finish before 3:00 p.m. if Sergeant Griffin could get Officer Woods in today. Rob just wanted to make sure that it was his signature on that report.

The judge looked at the prosecutor with a look like *that should be easy*, and appeared excited that this case could wrap up in a hurry. The prosecutor told him he'd have Woods there in less than an hour.

The jury was brought in and Rob called his first witness, Pam Cochran, a nurse from the hospital where Brent Colton was treated. After establishing the basics of her registered nurse status, her eighteen years of nursing experience, and the fact that she had no criminal record, Rob zeroed in on the reason she was in the courtroom on this date.

Rob asked her if she recalled a morning last July 5 during which she treated Brent Colton.

"Yes, I do," responded a noticeably nervous voice.

"Do you see him in the courtroom, today?"

"Yes, he is seated right there at the table," pointing to Brent.

"You don't really want to be here today, do you, Ms. Cochran?"

"No, I do not"

"However, you came here voluntarily, didn't you," asked Rob coyly.

"Yes," responded Cochran

"Would you now tell us, in your own words, sparing no detail, why you are here today?"

Cochran paused as if not sure where to begin. She took a deep breath and began. "In all my years of treating people, I have never witnessed anything close to what I witnessed that morning and it has bothered me every day and night since. As difficult as this is, I could not live with myself if I did not come forward. In the early morning hour, when the police officers arrived at the hospital, I had been treating Brent Colton. He was in rough shape and was extremely heavily medicated. I was concerned for his well-being. When the police officers went into his room and closed the door, I was alone at the nurse's station. We have a paging system in the hospital rooms, which allows us to listen to what is going on in the rooms. I was a little curious and a little nosy but most of all, I was concerned for my patient. I had been in the room minutes earlier trying to get his attention while I took vitals. He was completely out of it. I saw no value in the police interviewing a young man in a comatose state. I engaged the speaker system and listened."

By this time, Rob had positioned himself over by the jury box in an attempt to get the witness faced in that direction. It worked.

"Pam, do you recall what you heard as you listened through the speaker?"

"Yes, I do. I can't forget it."

"And do you have any other means by which you could recount what you heard as you sat at the nurse's station listening to the police officers?"

"Yes, I realized immediately that what was happening was very wrong—"

At that, the prosecutor jumped to his feet and objected to the witness characterizing the events as "wrong." The judge agreed and asked the jury to disregard the witness' opinion as to what she heard being "wrong."

I always loved it when a jury heard something and then was told to disregard it. In my opinion, it only made it more valuable to the defense. To call all this attention to a credible witness stating something was wrong and then make them pretend they never heard it...please.

Rob got her back on track. "What did you do as you listened to what went on in that hospital room?"

"I took notes."

"And do you have those notes with you today?"

"Yes, I do," she replied as she removed them from her white nurse's jacket pocket.

Once again, the prosecutor objected and a heated exchange took place before both sides were instructed to go to sidebar. The outcome was that Rob could ask questions and that if Pam needed to refresh her memory, she would be allowed to refer to her notes. As it turned out, the notes were not necessary because Pam recounted every detail of what went on in that room. The fact that the notes existed only served to strengthen Pam's credibility.

She explained through questioning that seconds after the door closed, she heard a man's voice say, "Well, well, Mr. Colton, we meet again. Rough night, huh? How was the big party?" to which there was no response, though she recalled the man chuckled in between his comments and questions. "Well the party's over, punk. No response, boy? You ignoring me? Maybe you'll notice me when I put you behind bars for twenty years, right where you belong. Watch and learn, Woods; this is how you take a confession."

The male voice, presumed to be Griffin based upon his comment to Woods, continued. "You have the right to remain silent, which you're doing a good job of for the first time in your life, and all that other shit I know you've heard before. Do you understand your rights, Colton?"

No response.

"I think I heard, yes, sir," Griffin said with a chuckle.

"Hey, Brent? Did you try to kill Quinn Charlton tonight? With your knife? Cause you hate him? Cause he was fuckin' your mommy?"

Again, no response but then Griffin said, "I'll put you down for a yes, yes, yes, and yes. I hope you're having sweet dreams 'cause you ain't gonna like where I'm sending you. C'mon, Woods, let's get out of here."

Cochran testified that she heard the hospital room door open and she immediately turned off the speaker. The police officers departed without saying a word to the nurse at the desk. When they were gone, she immediately went in to check on Brent, who was in a deep medication-induced sleep. Cochran attempted to get his attention by nudging him but was only able to elicit a moan-like grunt.

The courtroom was silent. Most of the eyes were on Sgt. Stanley Griffin, who sat completely motionless at the prosecutor's table. Pam Cochran was dismissed and made her way out of the courtroom. I whispered to Rob that I was going to secure Woods, who by now, we suspected was in the hallway outside the courtroom ready to testify that his signature was authentic.

The prosecutor requested a recess. The defense attorney argued vehemently against it and prevailed.

Rob stood and boldly stated, "The defense would like to call its next witness, Officer Peter Woods." The bailiff was sent to get Officer Woods, who I had found just entering the building.

"Good timing, Officer, they just called you as the next witness," I said. Then I couldn't help myself and added, "Don't forget, you're wearing the color of the law."

After being sworn in, Rob started in very calmly with Woods, but I knew he was fighting the ecstatic excitement of the moment. It was not often that you were served up a gift like he was about to uncover and open.

"Officer Woods, my name is Robert Bourque and I am the defense attorney for this young man, Brent Colton. I have a few questions for you today, a few very important questions that hopefully will clarify matters. Calling your attention to the police report that has been marked as Exhibit 3, would you please take a look at that and tell the jury if that is, in fact, your signature on page two?"

Officer Woods took the report handed to him by Rob, carefully looked at page one and then page two. He then lowered the papers and spoke very clearly into the microphone, "Yes, it is my signature."

Rob immediately responded, "By signing that legal document, are you authenticating the accuracy of the content of that report?"

With a slight hesitation, Woods replied, "Yes, sir."

"Officer Woods, I would like you to take a moment to carefully read that report to yourself. When you are finished, I have a few more questions."

Everyone in the room knew where this was going except Woods, thus the benefit of the sequestered witnesses.

After a minute, Woods again lowered the report as if to say, *I'm ready when you are.* Rob had again positioned himself next to the jury box so they could get a direct look and also to avoid Woods having any eye contact, whatsoever, with Griffin.

"Officer Woods, reminding you that you are under oath and wearing the color of the law, does that report accurately reflect the interview by Sergeant Stanley Griffin and confession by Brent Colton that took place in your presence on July 5 of this year?" By the time Rob finished his question, his volume and intensity had risen threefold.

Woods was on the hot seat and he couldn't hide it. The prosecutor stood and objected to the form of the question in an obvious attempt to buy Woods time and serve as a distraction. The judge snapped at him, "Sit down," and then realizing that there was a process to follow, said in a calm voice, "Overruled."

With all eyes on Woods, he leaned slightly forward and answered, "In my opinion, not exactly."

Not a bad response for a desperate situation, I thought. But I knew Rob was not going to let him off the hook.

"Why don't you tell all of us where it is inaccurate," snapped Rob.

After another objection to a question format, Rob agreed to take another route.

"Officer Woods, have you ever seen my client, Brent Colton, prior to today?" This was a layup and Woods appeared relieved as he responded, "Yes, sir."

And then in a loud and angry voice, "AWAKE?"

And then the "walk off."

"No, sir."

"So when you replied a moment ago that the report was 'not exactly' what went down, it wasn't even close, because Brent Colton was in a heavy medication-induced state of sleep, wasn't he?"

Woods had a response for this one, as he tried to dance. "I don't know what medication he was on, sir."

"Officer Woods, let me make this very easy for you. Did Brent Colton say one word that night in the hospital room when you and Griffin were there?'

"No, sir."

"So when you signed that report as a law enforcement official, you were not being truthful, were you?"

"No."

"So why did you sign it, Officer?"

"Because my supervisor told me to."

"And that supervisor...is that Sergeant Stanley Griffin, seated right over there?"

"Yes, sir."

Rob returned to his table and announced that was all he had for this witness at this time. The judge immediately called a recess and demanded that everyone remain in the courtroom with the exception of the jury, which seemed to leave reluctantly. They wanted to see what was going to transpire next.

What happened next is something I will never forget. Rob asked for not only a mistrial, but that all charges be dropped. He explained that if the defense were required to continue, we would hear from Brent Colton that he did not inflict the injury to Quinn Charlton that night. Brent had gone to his room to get his knife because he was in fear of a brawl that had broken out in his home. Upon returning to the scene of the fight, knife in hand, he observed people scattering quickly, leaving Quinn Charlton lying on the kitchen floor in a pool of blood. Brent went to him and kneeled at his side, setting the knife on the floor. At that moment, the police arrived.

And then to pile it on, Rob continued that the cut to Charlton's neck was actually inflicted by accident with a broken whiskey bottle as Charlton lunged at a man who was attempting to get Charlton to leave. That "man" had been an anonymous caller to my office; however, we were never able to get him to come forward. For obvious reasons, no one in Northshire, Maine, trusted the color of the law.

The judge granted the mistrial and subsequently ordered that all criminal charges against Brent Colton be dropped. The judge even spoke to him directly, apologizing for what he had been through at the expense of a severe wrongdoing that would not go unnoticed.

The judge did not take Stanley Griffin's actions lightly. He ordered the district attorney to place Griffin under arrest for obstruction of justice, filing a false report, and perjury. These amounted to felony charges; so Griffin was taken into custody and admitted into the county jail for processing, though he was allowed bail with conditions.

Due to a strong police union, he was not fired right away. Instead, he was immediately suspended pending further investigation. Public and media pressure did not afford the investigation to take more than three days, at which point Griffin was stripped of not only his rank and job, but also, via a consent agreement, he was banned from ever engaging in any form of law enforcement for the remainder of his life.

Stanley Griffin served a relatively short three months of a three-year jail sentence, but was on probation for five years, meaning that should he commit another crime during that five-year period, he would be returned to jail to finish out his sentence. He also paid a five-thousand-dollar fine and restitution to the state for its cost to bring this matter forward. The restitution was nearly seven thousand dollars. He then left the state, never to show his face in these parts again. Good choice, Stanley, because there was a line of people wanting to inflict their own justice upon you for previous despicable acts you had carried out.

As I was departing the courtroom after all the drama, I walked down the long marble floor hallway toward the exit. Sixty to eighty feet in front of me was Stanley Griffin, seated on a bench near the door with his hands behind his back. He was handcuffed and awaiting his escort to the nearby jail. I was alone; he was alone. I continued in his direction and as I got close to him, he looked up at me. I had nothing rehearsed so it just came out. I stopped and asked him, "How could you do that to someone's life?"

Without hesitation, he responded, "I was doing society a favor." And the way he said it made me believe that he truly believed that he had done the right thing.

I often wonder whether he ran into any of his old friends or victims of his belief system while incarcerated.

* * *

I wish I could say that it was uncommon; however, it is not uncommon to see law enforcement officials take the law into their own hands. On more occasions than I can count, I witnessed not only falsified confessions, but also relevant pieces of testimony and even physical evidence intentionally omitted or mysteriously lost, or found. I have struggled with this for a long, long time and have an opinion of how and why it occurs.

The criminal justice system is not perfect. It would be completely impossible to have a perfect system. It cannot exist, mainly because the system is set up to ensure that no innocent person is ever convicted. At the risk of not finding an innocent person guilty, many times, individuals who are actually guilty get acquitted. This is easily explained by the fact that our criminal justice system places a very heavy burden on the prosecution side. A prosecutor, whether it is a district attorney at the state level or a U.S. attorney at the federal level, must convince a jury of twelve people unanimously "beyond any reasonable doubt." That is a very tilted playing field. It is a daunting task, especially when a prosecutor may have hundreds of cases to handle while a defense attorney can spend many, often high-paid, hours conjuring up a defense. And the defense attorney wins if he or she can create even a slight belief of doubt.

Although I could never condone the action, I have come closer to understanding how law enforcement impropriety manifests in our system. The police officer or detective in the field investigates on behalf of the prosecution. More often than not, they get their perpetrator and arrest him or her, feeling certain that they have arrested the guilty person. Then the "imperfect system" kicks in and the individual the police *know* to be guilty walks. Frustration ensues and the vicious cycle begins.

I understand how the frustration rationalizes into justification to do what it takes to ensure a guilty verdict in light of the uneven playing field. I have good friends in law enforcement that I respect with my entirety. They are hard-working, civil-minded, and highly honorable people. Society owes them a large debt of gratitude for they certainly are not fairly compensated monetarily. I have spoken candidly with several of them about this issue and they have shed further light on the matter.

There is a strong sentiment among many law enforcement officials that defense attorneys and the private investigators that work on behalf of the defense are corrupt. The belief that the "other side" is "cheating" helps justify the behavior of "fighting fire with fire." The misconduct can spiral out of control, with the gloves off. It can sometimes parallel the Wild West and primitive days of justice.

With the spiraling out of control factored into the equation, the foundation of our system— to ensure that an innocent person not be found guilty, even at the risk of a guilty person being acquitted—is in great jeopardy. It is my strong belief that unfortunately no one is safe from this. I've seen it perpetrated on hundreds, including a completely 100 percent innocent neighbor. If you are not concerned and scared, you should be!

* * *

CHAPTER 5

STICKING YOUR NECK OUT

While finding and reuniting long lost loves or family members and working murder cases where you help prove a man's innocence are certainly more engaging, the truth of the matter is that the bread-and-butter work in the private investigation industry is insurance related. In order for me to lead the life I had become accustomed to, insurance investigation was the means.

In a nutshell, my marching orders were generally to determine the validity of an insurance claimant's alleged injuries. In the great majority of cases I was retained to investigate, there would be a claimant or alleged injured individual making a claim against a company, which may be self-insured or covered by an insurance company. Both sides generally had legal counsel who specialized in their respective positions of either plaintiff (injured) or defendant (company) representation. It was extremely rare—perhaps never—that an attorney would mix it up and have clients on both sides in different cases. Every now and then, an attorney would change his or her practice, not unlike the former prosecutor who becomes a criminal defense lawyer.

In addition to the parties and their lawyers, there is the medical profession's contribution to the equation. Just like there are attorneys who specialize in one side or the other, the same holds true in the medical arena. There are doctors well known to be plaintiff oriented, the ones who always diagnose and write a convincing medical report detailing the plethora of conditions or injuries, naturally caused by the incident or accident in question. The process allows each side to examine the claimant with a chosen medical professional. It is always amazing to me to read medical reports on the same individual, examined within a similar timeframe, that conclude with two very convincing opposite extremes. This highlights the profound degree of subjectivity within the medical profession and, in my opinion, not only takes many doctors off a pedestal, but also reduces them to greedy, immoral, and unprofessional with a level of integrity as low as any lowlife I ever experienced in the dredges of society. The money these people charge after becoming proficient on one side or the other is nothing short of criminal, in my opinion. Yes, either side of the legal battle could likely buy a medical determination no matter what the actual case may reflect. And just in case there remains any question, in my opinion, the extent of corruption within the medical profession within this arena facilitates the atrocities and ultimately costs you and me a lot of money.

So with the stage set and both sides digging in, what better than to discreetly and inconspicuously observe and document the activity in which these claimants engage when not in the confines of a doctor's office. How I love to refute these self-proclaimed, almighty, not-to-be-questioned authorities. If a picture tells a thousand words, the video must tell a million or so. It is hard to dispute a claimant doing something on video even when a doctor has just testified that, in his or her highly educated professional opinion, the individual is incapable of certain activity due to an injury. And I can attest that even the most pompous doctor can squirm in a seat as he or she watches the evidence play out!

* * *

"Ladies and gentlemen of the jury, sit back and enjoy the Randy Strout Show."

Randy Strout had been in a rear-end car collision with Randy being in the vehicle receiving the blow. He was alone in the car, which sustained over a thousand dollars of rear-end damage. There was no disputing the fact that Randy was hit and that he likely received a jolt resulting in a soft tissue injury. After nearly two years of chiropractic treatments as well as numerous medical examinations by both sides, his attorney filed a $350,000 personal injury lawsuit. According to Randy's medical experts, after two years of treatment, he had reached a medical recovery result of permanent impairment. He would never again have full range of motion, living with restricted mobility for the remainder of his life. Randy would experience chronic pain, though, according to his doctors, a small degree of relief could be realized by wearing a neck collar. Poor Randy.

The insurance company's doctors found absolutely no medical substantiation for his continued limitation; in fact, their medical professionals reported in carefully worded medical terminology that Randy was milking this alleged medical condition.

With the case steamrolling toward a courtroom showdown and the stakes pretty high, the insurance company contacted me with a request to conduct some undercover surveillance of Mr. Strout. When not in the controlled medical examination room, what was Randy up to? Did he, as stated in his claim, actually wear that collar and did he engage in physical activity that would corroborate one side's medical testimony or the other's?

In a worker's compensation case, where the claimant is injured in the workplace, there is generally considerable background information provided upon case intake. Many times, I was afforded the valuable opportunity to speak to an ally, perhaps from human resources, who would provide me with everything from photos of the individual I was to investigate to the person's known personal habits and hobbies. In a case like Mr. Strout's personal injury claim, I began my investigation not knowing much more than his name, address, a physical description, and that he was known to have had, in the past, a small painting business with a crew of three or four workers. He allegedly could no longer paint for more than a very short time on a very occasional basis.

After determining that Randy had a Ford pickup truck registered in his name, I started my work on this case by conducting a couple of late-night checks of the last-known residence we had on him. Sure enough, on both late-night drive-bys, the dark blue Ford pickup truck was parked in the driveway to the rented duplex situated a few homes in on a dead-end street off the main road. A survey of the area revealed a very easy environment in which I could remain inconspicuous and at the same time see Randy's vehicle emerge from the dead-end street.

On a seasonably warm October Friday morning, I initiated surveillance in the area. A drive-by of his road offered a brief glimpse of Strout's pickup truck without having to venture off Main Street. With his vehicle present and no outside activity at 6:30 a.m., I maintained surveillance from the parking lot of a nearby McDonald's. My thinking was that if Mr. Strout was engaged in painting, this was a perfect day to wrap up an exterior painting job, and this late in the fall, there was no guarantee how many opportunities remained.

His vehicle was unmoved all morning and there was no pertinent activity. He didn't appear to be getting a jump on the day, I thought. Patience was my mantra. I found it nearly impossible to believe that anyone capable of moving could choose to be inactive on a day like this.

One thing that seemed to stir activity was briefly leaving the scene of surveillance to use a bathroom or to grab a bite to eat. That lesson learned was why I packed a lunch in a cooler and was equipped with a plastic urinal "borrowed" from a local hospital.

All of a sudden...there he was. From fighting dead boredom and trying to stay focused to the adrenaline rush of seeing your subject on the move never failed to get my heart pumping. The pickup truck turned south onto Main Street being operated by a man exactly fitting the description of Randy Strout. He had shoulder-length hair, which did not hide the fact that he was not wearing a neck collar. The fact that he was not wearing the collar was not a big deal unless he claimed or testified that he always wore it, for example, when driving. Nonetheless, I snapped off a few photos of him while driving diagonally behind him and confident that I was in his blind zone.

I followed Strout for just over two miles and proceeded past him as he turned into a subdivision of single-family homes that was known to me to be a dead end cul-de-sac. In a case like this, which was on the court docket list and could be called for trial within the next few weeks, the last thing I wanted to do was get made, spook him, and thus, lose any opportunity to catch Mr. Strout engaged in physical activity. I maintained a roving surveillance in the area waiting for him to emerge from the subdivision.

After approximately thirty minutes, I was starting to feel like it was time to venture into the area in which he had turned. Just then, I observed Strout's vehicle exit the street. Randy was driving and a similarly aged man now rode in the passenger seat. In the bed of the pickup truck were several large speakers, guitar cases, another long case, as well as drums and microphone stands! *It's almost show time*, I thought.

Randy proceeded directly to a local bar no more than a half mile from his residence where he turned into the parking lot and out of view to the rear of the building. I quickly positioned myself in an adjoining rear lot where I started the video rolling. Within minutes, I was able to capture Randy as he bent, lifted, and moved the equipment from the back of the truck into the rear entrance to the bar. He moved quickly, exhibiting no sign of pain, discomfort, or limited mobility. With the truck emptied, I departed my surveillance position and drove into the front entrance of the bar/restaurant. I entered the establishment and inquired about making reservations for a party of eight to get a table in the lounge. I found out that the band played cover songs and started at 9:30 p.m. The manager escorted me to the bar area where I once again was able to observe Mr. Strout as he worked diligently moving speakers, hooking them up, and arranging monitor speakers and light columns. I reserved a table in the center of the room a couple of rows back from the front, thanked the manager, and departed.

After rounding up a small group of friends by offering free drinks all night, we gathered at the bar shortly after 9:00 p.m. and took our place at the second-row table. I positioned my camera equipment and myself with a clear vantage point to the stage, while my friends ordered drinks... two at a time! I didn't care, it was cheap cover and I knew the insurance company wouldn't mind either, especially if what I suspected was about to be captured on video.

When the band started at 9:45 p.m. (bands always start late), I was filming. It was more than I could have hoped for had I been able to write my own script.

Six weeks later…

"Mr. Strout, would you please remove your collar and demonstrate to the jury your range of neck motion," his lawyer asked with a dramatic flair.

With a slight grimace, Randy removed his padded collar and keeping his head straight, turned his stiff upper body toward the jury box. He then took a deep breath and slowly turned his head six to eight degrees to the right at which point he exhibited a pained look letting his audience know he could turn his neck no more. He then slowly returned to look straight ahead.

"Randy (now on a first-name basis for his sympathetic friends in the audience), I'm sorry to make you do this, as I know it is uncomfortable. However, before you put your collar back on, would you please attempt to move your head up and down in a nodding motion, as if you were trying to touch your chin to your chest…take your time."

Randy repeated his witness stand swivel, once again, to face the jurors. He then slowly lowered his chin no more than a couple of inches before closing his eyes and letting out a small grunt of discomfort.

"Thank you, Randy. I'm sorry to make you go through this necessary exercise. You may put your neck collar back on. Your Honor, could we take a brief recess to allow Mr. Strout to get comfortable?"

"I have no objection, Your Honor," said the lawyer for the insurance company. In fact, I have no cross-examination for Mr. Strout at this time though I may want to call him back to the stand after my witness testifies following the recess. Your Honor, may I request that my witness be able to set up his equipment during the recess so that we may proceed promptly upon our return?"

With that, the jury was excused and I went to work setting up.

After a twenty-minute recess and with the jury in place, the insurance company attorney was allowed to proceed. "I call David Smaha."

The attorney slowly and methodically questioned me, establishing my profession, license qualifications, and abundance of experience before raising his volume and pacing before the jury, "Mr. Smaha, do you recognize the man seated at that table (pointing to Strout)?"

"Yes, I do." (Notice, I answered the question twice, using only three syllables!)

"Have you in the recent past had occasion to monitor his activity?"

"Yes, I have."

"And without telling us what you saw, did you have the opportunity to document that activity?"

"Yes, I did."

"And was that in the form of video?"

"Yes, and still photographs as well."

"And this equipment you set up during the recess, does that prepare you to play that video for us here today?"

"Yes."

"Your honor, although I have further questions for my witness ("my witness," how cold), at this time I would like to request permission to play the video for which I have laid the foundation and then resume my line of questioning after it has played."

As the judge leaned forward to get just a little closer to my big screen premier, he offered his legal finding, "Granted; let it roll."

Knowing I already had a captive audience, I made my way slowly from the witness stand to the video controls. I wanted the anticipation to build. A brief glance to the jury to ensure that they received a direct view revealed intent eyes and bodies moved forward to the front edge of their seats. They were ready!

What happened next could only receive justice by enclosing the DVD as a part of every book. A picture tells a thousand words. This video told more than could be counted…

A spotlight pierced the dark stage and shined on a man standing with his back to the audience. Only the back of his head was revealed beyond a black cape, which was covering the man who had his arms outstretched and remained motionless. A few seconds later, the rapid and rhythmic beat of drums began, and on beat, the man rapidly moved his head fully forward at a near ninety degree angle and then abruptly jerked it back, hair flying over and over again at a fast pace. After thirty seconds of that, the jurors heard the addition of a lead guitarist accompanying the drums. The man then ran across the stage to the guitar player, all along being followed by the spotlight and keeping his back to the audience. Upon reaching the guitarist, the man leaned into the guitar so his head was inches away. As the guitarist blared a finger-flying lead solo, the caped man moved his head side to side keeping pace with every note played, with a full side-to-side motion.

Approximately thirty seconds later, the full stage lights went on and a keyboard player and bass guitarist completed the band's full sound. Then the caped man, who had made his way to the elevated area of the stage housing the drummer, leaped forward. As he turned in the air and landed directly in front of the center microphone stand, on which a harmonica was placed, his identity was finally revealed.

At the exact moment Randy's face appeared, I believe every single juror let out some sound, ranging from a gasping breath to bursts of laughter to one woman blurting, "Oh, my God!" The judge ordered everyone to be silent as the show continued.

Randy then removed the harmonica from its stand and proceeded to perform a highly spirited harmonica solo, once again revealing an abundance of full range and rapid head and neck motion. When the first song led directly into the second song, the judge asked me to pause the video. He then asked me how long the video ran, to which I responded two hours and thirty-eight minutes. He then thanked me and announced a recess, even though we were only minutes into a session following a recess. The jury was excused and upon their departure, the judge gave a firm urging that the matter get resolved between the parties within the next fifteen minutes...or else.

The judge disappeared to his chamber as the attorneys made their way to a side conference room. There we were, Randy and I, just the two of us, in this large and ominous courtroom, sitting about twenty feet apart. I knew exactly what I wanted to do in this situation...nothing. I had actually become competent at this fine art. I sat there pretty much motionless, enjoying the solitude.

Apparently, Randy had not mastered the art of "nothing." He broke the silence with a, "Hey, when this is over, and that might be pretty soon, is there any way I could get a copy of that DVD?" He didn't sound angry. He wasn't giving off any attitude. He appeared sincere in simply wanting a copy of the DVD. I turned to him and said, "Sure, I can get a copy for you." At that moment, the attorneys returned to the courtroom with stoic expressions. Randy's attorney spoke with him in a hushed manner. The attorney for the insurance company simply winked at me with an expression of satisfaction.

Within minutes, the judge peeked out from a curtain behind his seat. Seeing both attorneys present, he emerged and asked as he took his seat, "Gentlemen, have you worked it out?" Both attorneys, seemingly wanting to get credit for their joint effort, responded in the affirmative. It had been agreed upon that Randy would drop his entire claim in exchange for the insurance company's indemnification from pursuing him for insurance fraud...a clean split with both parties agreeing to let it all end right there, right then. The judge accepted the decision by approving it on the spot.

We all remained standing in the courtroom as the jury was marched back into its box. With brevity, as if he was late for his tee time, the judge explained that the case had been settled and, therefore, the decision of the jury was no longer necessary. He thanked them for their service and instructed them that they were permanently dismissed.

When the final juror was out of the room, the judge again slithered behind his curtain. The two attorneys gave their ritualistic handshake of brotherhood and I made my way to disassemble my equipment.

On my first trip to my vehicle to load up my stuff, I waited by the curb to allow an approaching vehicle to pass. Instead, it stopped and waved me across. I was halfway across and right in front of his truck when I realized that it was Randy. *Man, I hope this guy is stable,* I thought. I motioned him to remain stopped, reached into my briefcase, and removed the DVD. I handed it to him through his driver's window and said, "Here...I have a few other copies, and by the way, I'm a quasi musician myself, and I gotta tell you, you guys are tight; you sound awesome. Good luck with it." He thanked me and drove off.

* * *

CHAPTER 6

ONLY FOUR DAYS TILL CHRISTMAS

I imagine that plumbers and electricians must get the "I need a favor" call from their friends when they have a clogged drain or need something wired. I know lawyers who are always getting asked for free advice based upon their knowledge of the legal system. So it was no surprise for me to receive calls from time to time from friends in need of my services. I have several male friends who call me on a fairly regular basis.

"Dave, I just saw the most beautiful girl in the world and when I let her out of the parking lot at the mall, she smiled and waved. Can you run this plate? It was on a white Mercedes. I think I love her." I had him hold on while I punched it in and gathered a little information. "Here we go, she is thirty-one years old, she is five feet ten inches tall, blond hair, blue eyes, and she weighs, *holy shit*, only 125 lbs; she and her husband live in a home which is tax assessed at $2.4 million, and they have two small children. Her name is Alicia White and it says here that she is looking for love, happiness, and fulfillment from overweight forty-year-olds who are kind drivers. I think she loves you, too!"

* * *

It was a Wednesday evening, four days before Christmas. I was just about to sit down for dinner when I received a telephone call from an old buddy who now lived in New Hampshire. My first thought was *how nice that he is calling to wish me a happy holiday.* The tone of his voice quickly set me straight. He was distraught and immediately told me he needed help. I tried to put him at ease by telling him that I would do whatever I could to help. "Talk to me, what's going on?"

Mark had received a telephone call a few hours earlier from his wife, Susan, who was completely freaking out. She told him to get home as soon as possible and to save time to call her from his cell phone en route. Susan, a schoolteacher, explained that she had gotten home with their three-year-old daughter at 3:30 p.m. and retrieved the mail. They had received a bunch of mail including a small box wrapped in plain brown packaging paper. Opening the outer wrapping revealed red and white Christmas wrapping paper. Assuming a Christmas gift, she unwrapped it to find a small-corrugated brown box, nothing unusual until it was opened to reveal an approximate four-inch little blond-haired girl doll lying in a bed of white cotton-like packaging. Penetrating the doll from the front, heart area, right through the back, was a red plastic sword. There was an abundant amount of what appeared to be red paint simulating blood covering the doll's front side. Susan shrieked in fear. She and Mark were proud parents of a little blond-haired girl. The horror, fear, and terror Susan was feeling were immeasurable. Susan immediately thought to run and hide. She was frantically packing a bag for her and her daughter as Mark arrived home. Her parents lived in Rhode Island and she had decided that was where she would feel the safest.

Mark calmed his wife's immediate reaction. After getting their daughter safely situated watching a movie within eyeshot and only twenty feet away, they called the police. Fifty minutes later, the police arrived. After hearing the story and looking at the evidence, they made a determination. There was no return address so they really had nothing to go on…"so sorry."

My friend needed help. I could hear it in his voice. I got detailed directions to his new house and told him I'd be there in two hours. I also told him to keep his wife at home. I didn't want her leaving because she may hold a clue as to who and what was behind this heinous act. As I quickly packed a suitcase, I explained to my newlywed wife that I had to go. I extended to her the courtesy of explaining what I knew. It was the least I could do. *Why would anyone want to get involved with a PI?* I thought to myself. She proceeded to prepare my dinner for eating "on the road again." I ran out to my car with my suitcase and then ran back in the house to get my keys and my dinner. I don't believe more than ten minutes had elapsed since I hung up the phone with Mark.

It was dark outside when I arrived at Mark and Susan's home. As I turned into the driveway, Mark emerged from the backyard area holding a baseball bat. As amusing as he looked, I couldn't go there with him. He felt parental fear and he felt alone. He was not in a good place. If the intensity of the hug with which he greeted me was any gauge, Mark was extremely appreciative to have me there. As Susan emerged from the side porch entrance, I told Mark to get my bag out of the backseat while I hugged his wife. Susan was trembling and crying as she hugged me, and thanked me for coming. Mark yelling for the keys so he could get the bag out of the trunk interrupted us. Knowing that my trunk was full of equipment and wouldn't have even had room for a suitcase, I scolded Mark that if he was going to be my assistant then he should be able to find a suitcase in the backseat. As I peered into the car, illuminated only by a faint dome light, it hit me—an empty backseat. My suitcase was sitting in the driveway back home! I called my wife and asked her to look outside in the driveway and tell me what she saw. "Your suitcase," she replied as if there would be a follow-up question!

What could I say? I meant to do that? I didn't need it anyways? Instead, I told my wife to take it in so the neighbors wouldn't start any rumors about me being booted out! "Come on guys, let's get to work."

Mark was a stud and Susan was hot so it was no surprise to meet their absolutely beautiful little daughter, Brittney. As I looked at the doll, all

I could think was *what a sick fuck,* followed by *I'm going to find the bastard that did this.*

There wasn't much to go on. Through the years, I had developed a knack of quickly assessing what was presented and pretty much knowing in which direction I would be pursuing. Nothing was clicking. I had a brief thought about using this exact situation at an investigation seminar I would occasionally conduct. Twelve wannabe "investigators" would probably take at least eight different starting points. Without having much to say to these desperate friends of mine, I bought time carefully studying everything from the red and white Christmas wrapping paper to the brown corrugated box to the postmark to the little blond doll. The doll was not new and had been drilled with an electric drill to accommodate the plastic sword. I was assuming that the sender had an older daughter who had outgrown this particular toy and likely wouldn't have missed its disappearance. As I examined the doll, which was attired in a little sweat suit, Susan injected that their daughter was "always wearing sweat suits so whoever did this is close to us; they know us pretty well."

"Susan, you are likely correct that this sicko is known to you, which also contributes to the likelihood that they are not going to do anything beyond this. They want to scare you and they've done one hell of a job at that. Now, if they know you, then you likely know them, so it's time for you two to rack your brains. Who do you know that hates you? Think—recent spats at work, firings, jealousy, neighbor conflicts, money disputes, any legal proceedings, any social circle strains? I need you to brainstorm and verbalize anything that pops into your head."

Now, I know that if the tables were reversed, I could name numerous potential suspects, as I believe most people could. Mark and Susan didn't have many adversaries. They would occasionally come up with a name and then quickly dismiss him or her with "no way, not in a million years." Nonetheless, I was documenting their short list. After nearly thirty minutes of coming up with next to nothing, it was time for a little separation. There was no way that I was going to leave Susan alone with Brittney so I asked her if she would take a quick ride with me and lead me to a store where I could at least pick up a toothbrush, a razor, and a few other necessities. I knew there was a reason I left my shit back home! *Could I really be that clever*, I wondered, before quickly answering myself... *nah!*

As Susan and I drove to a nearby store, I reassured her that Mark and I were not going to let anything bad happen to anyone. I gave her my word on it. In order to uphold my end of the deal, I needed something in return. I told her I needed her complete 100 percent cooperation.

She immediately responded, "I know where you're going and I figured that was why you wanted to get me alone. David, I have already thought it through and I swear to you there is nobody. I lead a very mundane but content existence. I love my schoolchildren, and am very dedicated to teaching. I love my family even more. I have not done or said anything that I would not do or say in front of Mark. You know how badly I want to solve this horror; if I thought there was anybody in my personal life that may even remotely be capable or want to terrorize us, I would share it with you. I swear to you that the path to the person who did this does not start with anything I have going on. When you talk to Mark, let him know that all I care about is that we find out who did this. If he has done something that caused this, I don't care as long as we find out who is behind this so we can move on with peace of mind." Fighting back the tears, which eventually prevailed, she sobbed as she repeated herself that all she wanted was for this nightmare to go away. "I just want to wake up and have this be gone." I believed her.

When we got back to the house twenty minutes later, it was apparent that Susan had been away long enough. She hurried into the house and hugged her daughter as if she had just returned from Iraq. The tension and strain were not easing.

"Hey, Mark, your turn, can we go outside for a minute?" He didn't question me. Mark kissed his daughter who was being mesmerized by Barney and hugged Susan, assuring her that we would be right outside.

Same spiel, different result. Mark had thought this through and was ready with his response. Besides an employee of his small company he had terminated three months earlier and whom we had talked about in our joint brainstorming session, there was one other person who he thought was a long shot but just may be, possibly, demented enough to do something like this.

"I'm all ears, give it to me straight," I said.

Mark looked me straight in the eyes and without hesitation explained his situation. His twenty-four-year-old secretary and he had been working together, and at times very closely, for about ten months. Last summer, for the company outing, all the employees went on a dinner cruise ship on a full mooned, hot summer night. After a pretty wild night of drinking and dancing by everyone, Mark found himself slow dancing with Nicole. Before the song ended, Mark excused himself and departed the dance floor. He beelined to the boat's upper outdoor deck to avoid what he knew would be nothing but trouble. Mark broke stride in his story and said to me, "You know me, man; in the old days, I would have rocked that boat with her but I swear to you, I wanted nothing to do with it." A few minutes after leaving her on the dance floor, Nicole found him, this time alone. There was no one around to witness his or her mutual attraction. Mark claimed, and I believed him, that they talked for over a half hour and they never so much as hugged or kissed. On Monday morning, the awkwardness forced him into a behind-closed-door chat. He explained to her that he was married and that although she was beautiful, so was his wife and daughter, whom he loved and that he would never do anything to jeopardize his very happy life.

Recently, after several failed attempts at relationships, she stayed late at work and told him that she needed to talk with him. The "talk" turned out to be a guts spilling. She professed her love for him; she didn't care about the ten-year age difference; she wanted to spend every day of the rest of her life with him. Mark then confessed to an erroneous move by him. In an effort to make her go away but not wanting to hurt her feelings, he told her that he was attracted to her as well. Then he told her that if he didn't have a beautiful little girl he adored, then maybe things could be different... BUT he did, and that was that. For good measure, Mark threw in that his secretary was a little spoiled princess who would often gloat about the fact that she always got her way.

The ingredients were certainly there, I thought.

Mark asked what I was going to do. I told him to trust me.

I didn't want Susan to think that we were outside talking about situations that might have precipitated this terror, thus, creating more stress for these guys. As we entered the house, we were laughing about old times we had shared and then I got back on task. I told them together that they were leading boring lives, and though I was happy for them, I certainly didn't get any juicy stories. Although I wanted to hit the post office first thing in the morning, I wanted to exhaust or at least attempt to exhaust anything possible this evening. "The only name, the only suspect I can conjure up after talking with you two is... (I intentionally initiated a very long pause. I knew Mark's heart was pounding and I figured he was already thinking of his defense lines. Mark was a practical joker so I knew he'd appreciate the backside when I said) this guy you fired.

"I want to take a drive by his house so I'll need a little info. Susan, I'm done with you for now. Mark, I need you for just a few more minutes and then I'm going for a ride." With that, Susan carried Brittney to bed and as she left the room, Mark gave me a big smile that had an element of *you got me but I deserve it.* I told Mark, clearly outside the earshot of Susan, that I wanted info on both this ex-employee and this Nicole. Within five minutes, I had what I needed. I told them I'd be back in less than two hours.

Wanting to save the best for last, I located Mike Crandall's home first. It was a poorly kept ranch situated at the end of a dead-end road. The only light emanating from the house was that from a television in the front of the house. I didn't see what I wanted and there was nothing I was going to accomplish there.

Next, I drove to the north end of town and to the general area where Nicole called home. As I got close to her street, I started to see exactly what I was hoping for. Upon finding her duplex, I couldn't contain my "luck"—if that's what you call wearing plastic gloves and sorting through three twenty-something-year-old females' trash. "Yes," I blurted out, "tomorrow is trash day!"

Situated on the curb in front of Nicole's home were three bags of trash in town-approved yellow plastic bags. After circling the block and picking up three bags from another home, I did my old switcheroo. I had this gig down to about six seconds. As I pulled over, with one hand, I unloaded the replacement bags, and then in one continuous motion, picked up Nicole's three bags, tossed them in my car, and was off. Now the fun part.

In anticipation of getting lucky, I had Mark vacate his half of their two-car garage. There I was at 11:15 p.m. going through trash, one piece at a time. What I really wanted to find was red and white Christmas paper scraps matching the paper used on the mystery package. My luck had run out. That would have been way too easy and *that's no fun anyway*, I thought. It was time for bed.

The next morning I got up early with a fresh, rested mind. With a cup of black coffee, I sat at the dining room table and studied the limited evidence. I knew my first, and quite frankly my best shot (granted a long shot) was a visit to the local post office. This package had been sent from the main post office in Manchester, New Hampshire. I had a vision of the tens of thousands of packages that were being sent this time of year. The thought that this may never get solved entered my mind, but I quickly tried to erase it—positive thinking. One thing may lead to another.

There was also an emblem on the corrugated brown box identifying its manufacturer as Weyerhaeuser & Company. I knew that they were the largest manufacturer of boxes in the country but that was about all I knew. The emblem revealed that they were located in Oregon.

My trip to the post office proved useless. I got a chance to speak with the postmaster who was in a mind-set to fend off the sharks. The local media was there doing their annual story about last-minute shoppers and this was his annual moment of glory. He was decked out in his best suit, ready with rehearsed lines and chuckles for his upcoming interviews. My subtle threat to steal his thunder and get the media focused on my story prompted him to cooperate a little. He had his assistant provide me with the names of all the clerks who worked on the day the package was sent, and as they took their breaks throughout the morning, I was given an opportunity to ask them whether they had any recollection of the package in question. My thinking was that just possibly the absence of a return address might trigger something. I was wrong, and shortly before noon, I was back in my car driving aimlessly.

I kept thinking that the red and white Christmas wrap was one of my best opportunities in this case, so I decided to get into my only two suspects' homes—not break in, just get inside for a quick look. Barring a surprise Jewish intervention, I believed it was a given that my suspects' households would have Christmas trees with presents underneath.

Using pretexts of investigating a matter in the area, I was easily able to get into Mike Crandall's home and sit with him in his living room. Although there were not many gifts under his silver Christmas tree, none revealed the paper I so wanted to find. After being told that neither he nor anyone in the household heard anything suspicious just after midnight two nights ago, I probed a little deeper. Not only did he have two sons, his only grandchild was a little boy. This guy was falling to the bottom of the two-person suspect list very quickly.

Getting into Nicole's home could be a little trickier, I thought. She would be at work. Her roommate was a waitress and would most likely be home alone. The belief and truism that you really only get one shot prompted me to pull out an old trick. I went to my trunk and got a gift-wrapped one pound box of chocolate, printed a card to Nicole from a secret admirer. I figured she had many secret admirers or at least she likely believed she did. I wrapped it in plain brown paper, thinking two can play this game, got dressed in my UPS uniform, prepared my clipboard, placed the magnetic signs on the sides of my car and I was off.

I pulled up in front of the residence and hurried to the front door like any delivery person does, especially at that time of year. A very, very attractive female in her twenties came to the door attired in a T-shirt and sweatpants. I asked if she was Nicole to which she responded that Nicole was at work but that she was her roommate. I gave a puzzled look to my clipboard, threw in that this was only my first week on the job, and said that I had a package for Nicole and that the instructions said that she had to sign for it. "Oh, it's OK, I'll sign for it, Nicole would want me to," she said with a smile to comfort me. I responded that I didn't think I was supposed to as I gave a little squirm. Now for the closer, I thought.

"I'll make a deal with you. I'll leave you the package if you sign Nicole's name on line nine and if you let me use your bathroom. I've been drinking coffee all morning."

"Deal," she said with a smile, "the bathroom is right around the corner before the kitchen."

All I could think about as I headed to the bathroom was that she let me in way too easily. I almost wanted to admonish her and let her know that there are freaks out there and how careless it was to let a stranger in her home, especially looking like she did, but I had a job to do and I wanted to remain on task. I quickly did my business and returned to the entry door through the living room where I hoped to find the girls' Christmas tree. Unlike Mike Crandall's tree, there were lots of gifts either for or from the girls; however, once again, no sign of the red and white paper I so wanted to match. I wanted to go home but there was no way I could until I did anything and everything possible.

I looked at the limited evidence again, hoping I had missed something during the previous ten times I studied the stuff. On nearly every corrugated cardboard box, you will find a box manufacturer's certificate on the bottom, which reveals the company that made the box. Most of them are either from Weyerhaeuser & Company or Georgia-Pacific Corporation. In addition, it gives dimension, construction requirements per freight classification, edge crush test rating for shipment capacity, and a bunch of useless information...which explains why you likely have never paid much attention to the markings. It also will generally have some code stamped within the emblem like a certificate denoting the boxes identity to the manufacturer. On the bottom of this box was G567-937562008. I got the telephone number to Weyerhaeuser in Oregon and placed the call.

All I could think of was the fact that it was three days before Christmas and I was calling a place of business on a wild goose chase. After penetrating the front line receptionist and learning that I needed to speak with someone in product development, I felt like I was beginning to get lucky. What I learned next was more than I could have hoped for in a million years. The box had been a special order for a mail order catalog company in North Conway, New Hampshire. Although I was ready to play the card that I was a detective working on a very time-sensitive criminal matter and more than willing to e-mail or fax my credentials, I never had to. The young man who took my call never questioned my need to know. Instead, he just offered everything he could. The order for this box had come from The Olde House Art Supply Company and only four months earlier, near the end of August. There were only one thousand made and his information suggested that the box was constructed for the purpose of shipping a craft paint set. He added that one thousand was the minimum number in special order box dimensions. I got his name, Carl, and thanked him profusely; I actually felt good for a minute.

The Olde House Art Supply Company had been around for over a hundred years and I think the lady I ended up speaking with was there when they first opened their doors! In light of the fact that the older generation has a much higher degree of respect for law enforcement (not that I was law enforcement) than the younger generations, I opted to take the route of mistaken identity. I took control of the call by asking her name and then informing her that I was a detective in Manchester, New Hampshire (true), working a case of criminal threatening upon a child and that I would sincerely appreciate her assistance. "Madeline" was unbelievable. She corroborated the box manufacturer's information and stated that her computer revealed 840 boxes in stock. After throwing in a "God bless you" and a "you are going to make Christmas joyful again for a little girl," Madeline offered her ability to do a run on that piece. In a nutshell, she could print off a detail of every consumer who purchased that catalog item. With my sincere thanks, I asked her to fax that list to the "station," providing her with Mark's company fax number. Within seconds, I was on my way to his office and had Mark anxiously standing by his fax machine. There was anticipation that closure could be on the horizon.

It was approximately ten minutes from the time I hung up with Madeline to the time I arrived at Mark's office. During that time, Mark received the fax of one hundred sixty names and had immediately scoured it. To his extremely pleasant surprise, he immediately knew who had sent the package. One name stood out on the list. It was Brian Bailey who was his fraternity brother ten years earlier in college. The escalation of practical jokes in the frat house had escalated to intense animosity, jealousy, and hostility...ten years ago. Nothing had happened for over a decade until...Mark, Susan, and Brittney had all attended the ten-year anniversary of his college graduation during Homecoming weekend this past September. While there, Mark and his family were photographed and subsequently profiled in the "Success Stories" section of the college magazine. I had little doubt that Brian Bailey read about Mark, his successful family, and thriving business—in which he helps the handicapped. It was too much for him to ignore and, thus, the threatening package. Oh yeah, in the magazine photograph, Brittney was in her pink sweat suit!

Mark was enraged more than any man I had ever laid eyes on. I begged him to calm down and he did, a little. I even had to throw in a "You owe me, man; now calm the fuck down." It was for his own good.

After a fabulous dinner, I had to get back to my family. My "number of shopping days until Christmas" had been reduced to hours. Mark had decided not to go to the police, but instead handle it in his own manner. After all, he hadn't been very impressed with their initial role in this matter. I begged him not to do anything stupid, which would only potentially allow this asshole to prevail. Mark was very smart. I had no doubt about him being able to handle the situation. The important thing was that the origin of the threat was known, and not felt to be real or dangerous.

There is no way to adequately describe how good I felt driving home. To be able to take a horrific situation, defuse it, and allow a close friend to enjoy the holiday with his family was probably the greatest gift I could wish for.

All I asked in return from Mark was for him to never tell me what he would do to this asshole blast-from-his-past. He never did and I'm good with that.

* * *

CHAPTER 7

ONE WORD CHANGES EVERYTHING

I don't remember much about the case. It was a court-appointed criminal matter and I had limited authorization for funds. That was all right, and very typical, because it was just a matter of conducting a single interview. I was provided discovery, which was basically a police report containing a woman's brief statement. My investigation was a matter of interviewing this person who happened to be the only witness to some incident about which I have no recollection. This type of case was like a broken record. Did the statement reflect what the witness had actually told the police, and just as important, was there any additional information, either conveyed (that didn't find its way into the report) or yet to be conveyed that would shed additional light upon the incident?

Although I can state with certainty that I never once identified myself as a police officer, that does not mean that I was never perceived as such—go figure.

On this date, I trimmed my moustache, hopped into my Ford LTD sedan, attired in dark pants, a dress shirt, and navy blazer...and sunglasses. I knocked on the door to the apartment and was greeted by a woman in her thirties who, fortunately, just happened to be the subject of my interview. *So far so good,* I was thinking. After confirming that she was my girl, I flashed my photo license, which bore a state seal, and waved a copy of a police report, which also contained a state seal, as I stated, "Ma'am, I am so sorry to have to bother you again on this, but I need to review your statement with you. The good news is that it may prevent this case from going to trial, so may I step inside? This should only take a minute or two." Slam dunk, I'm in.

As I entered the small, dark, dungy apartment, I couldn't help but think, *I want to get out of here...* little did I know. The apartment was small with one approximately sixteen-by-eighteen-foot room that served as the entryway, living room, dining room, and kitchen. I assumed there was a bedroom through a far doorway.

My entrance had caused a large colorful cockatoo to become very loud and agitated within its cage across the room. A young girl, I figured to be about six or seven, had moved from the couch in front of a blaring television to the cage and was telling the bird to calm down. The woman explained that the bird didn't like men. I responded that I was not offended, especially because I was not very fond of birds.

I think it was the combination of the pungent odor within the apartment and the incessant loud squawking of this flapping parakeet on steroids that had me working quickly. Little Suzy was not succeeding in quieting the caged beast.

I was just about finished with the formality of confirming this woman's statement when she glanced over toward the cage. As if to remind little Suzy, the woman said, "Don't let her out of the cage." With a questioning look on her face, Suzy responded. Apparently, through the loud squawking, Suzy didn't hear the first (and most important) word of her mother's command. Before another word could be uttered, Suzy whipped open the side cage door and set this flapping creature free. Not to sound like a "fish story," but this thing had a three-foot wingspan and set flight to a far corner of the room before targeting the only man in the room. The woman immediately screamed at me, "Hold very still and let it land on your head." That was not the natural response I had in mind.

With a pointed beak, claws extended, and screeching in an unfriendly tone, it was headed right for me. The concept of standing still just didn't feel right and was quickly excluded as an option. It felt so surreal, as everything seemed to shift into slow motion.

As the gigantic (it sure looked gigantic as it moved to within a few feet from my head) bird closed in on me, I felt like I was down to one option. Now, for all you PETA animal lovers, you may want to skip ahead to the next chapter.

In baseball, you get three strikes. I knew I'd only get one. I grabbed my leather bound notebook with both hands. With the bird two feet from my head, I swung at the high and tight pitch. I might have closed my eyes as I swung, but I knew I hit it not only by the feel of the contact but also by the squelch of a wild animal being attacked. I got my feet under me to note the whereabouts of the staggered but durable bird, a good ten feet "down the line," which gave me enough time to bolt out the door. *Let it land on your head,* I chuckled to myself.

Interview over. *Cage closed!*

* * *

CHAPTER 8

MIXED SIGNALS

I guess…no, I know; I gave the wrong signal.

It was just another routine documentation of an insurance claimant's activities. An anonymous tip had been provided to an insurance company that a self-proclaimed bedridden individual was working daily and actively as a high school assistant football coach. My job was simply to document, with still photos and video, this individual engaged in any physical activity related to his role as assistant coach…easy.

The team practiced in an inner-city park that was made up of several baseball, football, and softball fields, volleyball, tennis, and basketball courts, as well as an outdoor stage for entertainment, a large playground, and a large duck pond complete with a center fountain. A one-way paved circular road that ran around the entire park accessed the park. Parking was plentiful as all along the road, there were multiple vehicle parking areas where one could pull off the road closest to a desired activity. Many people would back into the spots and sit in their cars to watch the activities, which made it very easy for me to be inconspicuous.

Shortly after 3:00 p.m., I entered the park and observed a football team engaged in practice. Within minutes, I was able to back my vehicle into a parking spot that afforded an inconspicuous vantage point of the practice field area. I got my camera and video equipment turned on and ready as my eyes perused the activity some one hundred feet away, down a small hill, and through a spattering of large oak trees. It didn't get much better or easier than this. There was occasional activity in the immediate area consisting of a few walkers and a car or two passing by every few minutes.

The photos provided to me for identification purposes made the next step a slam-dunk. There he was, attired in T-shirt, shorts, and cleats. There was a whistle around his neck, which he used repeatedly to signal the next group of linemen to block into and move an iron-padded sled on which he stood, getting jarred each time the players made contact.

After getting a few still photographs and some video, I realized that a better vantage point existed twenty feet back on the one-way road. Though I was tempted to disregard the one-way aspect of the road, I didn't want to draw any unnecessary attention. I waited for a car to pass by and then circled around the entire park and repositioned myself. It took longer than it should have because the guy that I had let pass by crept around the entire route before parking right where I had been minutes earlier.

I backed into a great spot only to find my coach no longer engaged in the sled banging. Better yet, he was now serving as quarterback as receivers and defenders ran pass routes. This was getting better. The only problem was that where I was now situated was not the best vantage point. If only I had stayed where I had been—frustrating.

I needed to move only a short distance so I pulled out again. Just before I came upon my ideal space, another car I had let pass by me slipped into the spot, leaving me with no other options but to make the loop. The good news was that a glimpse in my rearview mirror revealed asshole number one now departing my original parking spot. I proceeded to zip around the loop and was able to get into my original parking spot, which was right where I wanted to be in order to document my boy.

As I was getting situated and ready to roll the video, the guy who had just departed the space circled by me and smiled. I swear I didn't reciprocate with a smile. In fact, I acted as if I did not see him at all.

Within minutes, I started videotaping my coach. Out of the corner of my eye, I saw this same guy approaching my vehicle on foot. Damn. I set the camera down and lowered my window a bit, as he headed right for me. I was thinking, *What the hell does this guy want?*

He smiled and said, "Hi," as he neared my car.

I said nothing, to which he responded by opening his jacket to expose the upper part of his sweatpants, revealing a very pronounced raging erection. He grabbed himself and uttered something to the effect of "I'm obviously ready, are you?"

Holy shit. I didn't see that coming.

I immediately ordered him in no uncertain terms to get the hell away from me. He acted surprised.

"What's your problem?" he asked, as he turned and slowly walked away. Then he said the words that would resonate…"If you didn't want me, then why did you give me the signal?"

After he left, I resumed my work and got the evidence I needed all the while trying to figure out what had just transpired. I would later realize that my normally steady video hand was not as steady as usual.

In this case, as well as nearly everything in life, it eventually became clear.

The park was an established hangout for homosexual men. Someway and somehow, a system had been established. By backing your car in and then driving behind someone around the loop of the park, and then being followed after allowing the other vehicle to park, constituted "the signal." In my unknowing and innocent attempt to ascertain the most advantageous vantage point to gather evidence, I had given the signal.

First, I followed him around the loop. After parking ever so briefly, I looped again, this time allowing him to reciprocate and follow me and then nearly consummated the deal by backing into a space near or at the original starting point.

But we hadn't even spoken and he was ready to get it on. I couldn't help but wonder if there were similar "signals" about which I had no knowledge within the heterosexual world. In the months and years that followed, I would occasionally drive by the park and notice vehicles looping around the one-way road right behind the other usually riding right up the ass of each other.

* * *

CHAPTER 9

IT'S A DOG-EAT-DOG WORLD

In a profession where I concede that routine is the norm, this one certainly seemed to fit the mold. The call was from a local attorney, Brent Shortill, with whom I had done a ton of routine insurance surveillance. As soon as I heard his voice, I reached for an insurance intake form. However, this time it was not the case!

Brent seemed pleased to inform me that he had something a little different for me. He represented a client who had a judgment against an individual for several hundred thousand dollars. Getting a judge or jury to say, "You win" and the other side owes you is often only half the battle. It's all about collecting the judgment.

In this matter, Brent's client, a publishing company in Los Angeles, had secured the first half of the equation, but was having trouble collecting. The defendant, Tommasso Salvatore, had received a three-hundred-thousand-dollar advance for a proposed writing project. Mr. Salvatore was a proven published author, having written several well-known and controversial books. He had lived a colorful life, to say the least. I was informed that Salvatore had been on the lam for years. After working undercover for the CIA, Mr. Salvatore supposedly was to write an exposé novel centering on a world-renowned Middle Eastern terrorist who, for security reasons (mine), will remain nameless. As Salvatore began his project, he was tipped off that someone wanted to stop his writing, and not in a polite manner! He believed from reliable sources that assassins had been given marching orders to eliminate him. I did not consider that to be a stretch based upon his background and intended endeavor. The publishing company got stiffed when Salvatore bolted. The publishing company had a tip, a hunch, or some belief that Mr. Salvatore and his wife had settled, at least temporarily, in southern Maine.

My job was simply to attempt to determine if there was any information out there to corroborate the belief he was in my "backyard." I asked if it was possible to speak with, even anonymously, whoever started this lead process. Inevitably, there is more information available from initial sources, though nearly invariably they believe that they have nothing of value to add.

"Not much to go on, Brent, how about a budget?" He was ready, "Don't you have that guarantee find fee deal where for a flat fee you locate someone, and if you don't find them, there is no charge?" Wow, this one would certainly challenge what had been a very decent and lucrative program for years. The FBI had been looking for this guy for two years, as technically he had moved across state lines after absconding with a substantial amount of money. Brent was a good client and a friend. "Sure, Brent, five hundred bucks if I find him, nothing if I don't. What have you got for me?"

All I really had was Mr. Salvatore's full name, date of birth, social security number, and the Wisconsin plate registration of a dark green Toyota Camry he had been connected to over a year ago. I also had his wife's data and the fact that they likely still have a little white dog, which they treated like their kid since they had no children. Now you may think, a little white dog, big deal! However, I valued every little tidbit in matters like this. If that kid/dog got sick, they would be going to a veterinarian, and let's face it, if you can't get info out of a vet office, you don't deserve to keep your private investigator's license. In addition, the dog aids in the identification process. If I ever find this guy, it certainly would support positive identification if I see him walking a little white dog.

I hung up the telephone, let out a sigh, and wondered if I should even try. After all, the FBI, a well-funded terrorists' assassin, and God knows who else either had been or were continuing to hunt this guy down. Mr. Salvatore knew how to hide; he was somewhere tucked away in a corner of the United States—in southern Maine! He figured that he was safe there and I figured he was probably right.

I conceded to go through the standard motions and check public records—maybe I could get lucky and find a ticket for speeding or operating an unregistered vehicle. If this guy had led the life it appeared he had, then defying the little laws was probably to be expected. NOTHING—the trail wasn't cold, it didn't exist. This guy wasn't flying below the radar; he was invisible.

I needed to get lucky. I always said that it was better to be lucky than good; ideally you're both. To continue with my "standard operating procedure," I called my contact at the phone company. "Hey, Betty Lou (not her real name!), can you check a name for me? It may be a new listing...go statewide and check his and her name, published and non-published." After a few seconds, she reported, "Nothing published." That was no surprise. "Nothing non-published either," still no surprise. PI Tip of the Day: Silence is golden! People hate silence so that's what I would give my sources. Instead of accepting closure or letting them off the hook by saying good-bye, I would say nothing. "Wait, I may have something. I just ran her name without the last name, the hyphenated name... likely her maiden name...and there is a six-week-old non-published listing for her."

I asked if it was in southern Maine and Betty Lou snapped back, "David, you know that I can only tell you so much. There are strict federal regulations about privacy relating to non-published numbers"—Not as if I hadn't heard that speech before. "I know; I'm sorry for asking. Thanks, Betty

Lou… hey, how about a drink some time; I miss you. I'm meeting some friends tonight at 5:00. If you get a chance, stop by and I'll buy you a drink."

"I can't tonight but thanks, maybe some other time; you know it's busy being a single mom."

"Well, take care and I hope to catch up with you before Christmas.

At 5:10 p.m., Betty Lou turned into the parking lot just as previously arranged. Yes, there was an "arrangement." We had previously discussed the possibility that the telephone company not only could, but also did monitor calls. As a measure of precaution and to preserve her employment (and, therefore, my well-cultivated information source), nothing confidential was ever to be communicated telephonically.

I was sitting at our corner table by the window, the same one I had been at for every one of our previous several dozen meetings, as she entered the bar. In a word, Betty Lou was "extremely hot" (OK, two words). It never failed to entertain me watching her entrance. Dozens of men in a bar after work and none of them ever seemed concerned about getting caught looking. Betty Lou was five feet ten inches tall, long legged, thin, blond, and very well proportioned. She would take a step into the bar and stop. She would then remove her sunglasses; give a little shake of her shoulder-length hair (as if fixing it) and pause, as if not being sure where she would settle. I never challenged her on it, but there was no doubt in my mind that she loved being noticed and giving every turned head in the room a moment of hope that she was there with no direction. The truth of the matter was that I was always in the same spot, though she would act out the old *oh, there you are* expression and proceed to glide across the room.

At this particular meeting, Betty Lou didn't take her seat. "I'm sorry, I can't stay. My daughter just called me and has to go back to school to get her backpack that has her homework...yada, yada." She handed me a folded piece of paper, leaned over, gave me a peck on the cheek, and took off. Score! As much as I loved to look at her, the drink and the conversation were all part of the work product. I had so many cases that needed attention, as well as reports to be dictated and billed. I was good, really good with her inability to stay. After all, as much as I would have loved to love Betty Lou, I knew that it would jeopardize, in fact, eventually obliterate an incredibly valuable information source. And without sources, I was nothing.

Through the years, I developed special friendships with not only Betty Lou at the phone company, but several contacts at the U.S. Postal Service, law enforcement agencies, judge's clerks, state workers in nearly every department (Labor, Motor Vehicles, Workers Compensation, Vital Statistics, Human Services, etc.), the power company, the cable company, the three major network news departments, reporters at the local papers, and the list goes on. Nothing like pictures of Benjamin Franklin to solidify "friendships!"

I shoved the paper in my pocket, dropped a ten-dollar bill on the table, and bolted out of there. As I was driving back to my office, I removed the paper from my pocket and unfolded it. In a way, I was looking at five hundred bucks. My "guarantee find" fee was still intact! Mr. Salvatore and his wife appeared to have settled into a residence in an area of Kennebunkport I was familiar with, familiar enough to know that the homes in this area were very large and just happened to be very near Walker's Point, the summer home of President George H. W. Bush.

I had received the assignment only six hours before, but there was no way I would let my client know I was done. Despite the fact that we had a deal, $500 to locate him or no charge, inevitably, a client would feel ripped off if they knew how quickly I had accomplished the task. In addition, I was going to be in the exact area of the residence in two days, so I figured I'd throw in a free drive-by into my report.

Sure enough, an eight-bedroom, three-story mansion located on a moderately traveled street that eventually led to the Atlantic Ocean—the high-rent district. I observed no outside activity as I conducted an early evening drive-by. Parked in the driveway on the side of the residence next to a set of stairs leading to a large wraparound porch was the Toyota Camry with Wisconsin plates. Now, it's invoice time! Thank you, Betty Lou!

To say my client was happy was putting it very mildly. Five hundred bucks and three days later, the publishing company president was ecstatic. He used an expression that his appetite was not fulfilled with an appetizer alone. Legal wheels went into motion, and within a day, my telephone was ringing for additional services, specifically to serve Mr. Salvatore in hand with a subpoena. The subpoena would command his appearance in a federal court to answer questions regarding the payment of the judgment as well as all of the added fees to track him down and get his ass into a courtroom.

Even though I was speaking to him on the telephone, I could tell that Attorney Brent Shortill had a smile on his face as he asked if another five hundred dollars would guarantee subpoena service. I professionally suggested a five hundred dollar budget, and, as he knew, if I could get it done for less, I would only invoice for time expended.

On a cool and beautiful October morning, I proceeded to Mr. Salvatore's residence, arriving there just after 7:00 a.m. I could not imagine anybody remaining indoors on a day like this. After a few drive-bys at thirty miles per hour on a twenty-five mile per hour posted road, and only casual glances with my eyes, not turning my head, I determined that there was no outside activity. The Toyota Camry was present in the driveway and seemingly unmoved from where I had observed it several days earlier.

I was able to locate a church parking lot about 150 yards away from the residence from which I could inconspicuously view the front of the house as well as, more importantly, where the driveway met the road. Pay dirt would be to follow the vehicle to a local store or public place, snap a few photographs of him entering an establishment (maybe even with that little white dog), and serve him upon his return to his vehicle. I could hope!

I sat in my vehicle for over five hours before anything occurred. Shortly after 1:00 p.m., I observed a small white dog sniffing his way onto the front lawn probably no more than twenty feet from the porch. Within one minute, the dog was out of view and a drive-by several minutes later revealed no outside activity, whatsoever. At the very least, I felt confirmation that Mr. Salvatore was here and the dog had to go out from time to time. It was also evident that the door used by my subject was the side door, which was just a few steps to his vehicle door. This was starting to take on a look of difficulty. I returned to my spot, lowered the seat so that my line of vision was through the upper steering wheel opening. I removed my shoes and got comfortable. To effectuate my desired result, this was going to require patience.

Although I had completed a billable day by midafternoon, I felt like staying. My thinking was that the longer someone stayed inside, the more likely I was closer to seeing him or her depart. Nonetheless, with no activity by 6:30

p.m., I conducted one last drive-by, saw nothing, and headed back to my office.

With commitments to another matter the following day, I placed a call to my client and briefed him on my findings. As if the publishing company was going to give up with less than a thousand dollars expended. I suggested a little creativity and Brent wholeheartedly agreed. I would let a few days go by and initiate Plan B.

Dating a private investigator can't be a lot of fun. It's not as if you go home when the whistle blows. It's not even as benign as sometimes working a little late at the office. After saying good night, I may depart at 5:00 a.m. only to follow someone to Atlantic City and stay for a few days. "Sorry I missed the dinner party or maybe even your birthday, we'll celebrate when I get back." "I don't know when that will be; you know that." The cute little blond I was seeing at the time of this case would later become my wife. I'm glad I didn't sugarcoat the requirements of my job. Thankfully, she seemed to embrace it, especially when I could include her!

Renee and I skipped church that Sunday morning, and headed out in separate vehicles. I drove a different vehicle than I had used previously in this matter "just in case." With no early morning activity, apparently, Mr. S was playing hooky from church as well; we went into action on Plan B. A quarter mile east of the residence, Renee and I pulled over to the side of the road and let the air out of her right rear tire. She then proceeded on the road to a predetermined spot diagonally in front of the residence. After pulling over and getting out of the car, Renee played out the drama of discovering the flat. She stood, looked, and then lifted the rear hatch of the car and removed the spare. I was taking it all in with binoculars out of view of the residence. Renee loved to get dolled up so she loved this. Attired in a short black and white polka dot dress and four-inch heels, she actually started to attempt to loosen the tire bolts, but to no avail. After a pause, she slowly approached Salvatore's front door and rang the doorbell. No response. After a second ring, Renee heard through a small speaker by the door a male voice coarsely ask, "What do you want?" Renee timidly replied, "I have a flat tire and I was wondering if you could either help loosen—"

"Go away."

As an experienced PI girlfriend, Renee rang the doorbell again but received no response. Mr. Salvatore was not about to fall for a PI 101 trick.

After walking up the road, well out of view and meeting me for a can of "fix-a-flat, we had lunch. Renee returned to her vehicle ninety minutes later, pumped up the tire and departed. We played it out always suspecting that a justifiably paranoid man was observing her.

It had been so easy to find him yet it was unfolding to be quite a formidable task simply to hand him a piece of paper.

After discussing my latest attempt with Brent and the publishing company via conference call, I became aware of the intense feelings of the president of the company. He wanted Mr. Salvatore's ass and it was professed that money was no object. I sensed that it was not only business, but personal as well. The fact that they had finally and inexpensively located their guy and were now a subpoena service away from landing him in court was simply not a position to squander. The words carte blanche were used to express the strong desire to get this service completed.

It had become abundantly clear that Mr. Salvatore was not going to fall for any cheesy trick to lure him out of his sanctuary. And the last thing we wanted to do was spook him into uprooting and departing. It was back to basics, good old surveillance.

Over the next week, I conducted surveillance for four long days. Very little was revealed. A woman, presumed to be his wife had departed in the Toyota Camry, alone in the vehicle. I followed her to a local grocery store where she purchased a dozen items before returning directly to the residence. The only other activity was the occasional letting out of the little white dog. This seemed fairly ritualistic and seemed to occur only a couple of times a day. Mr. Salvatore would emerge from the residence, go down the side stairs, and stand in the driveway between the car and the porch. I figured that any attempt to approach the house or drive into the driveway would undoubtedly result in his retreat to safety, which he could accomplish in a matter of ten seconds or less. In addition, a failed attempt would spook him beyond repair and negate the progress we had made in locating this guy.

At some point, and I wasn't sure when, this case had become sport. It was now about the challenge of prevailing. No longer did I care about how long it was taking or how many hours were being billed out. I was intent on serving this bastard one way or another.

I didn't know what day it was; however, it was at least eight days later because I was back in the vehicle I had used the first day I located his residence. I had exhausted my fleet of surveillance vehicles. Just as had occurred on every previous day, the dog was let out and I observed him sniffing around the driveway. On this date, unlike previously, the dog extended its normal perimeter and continued down the entire seventy-five-foot driveway at a moderate pace. It all happened so fast after the countless hours of inactivity. My heart rate increased as I sat up (though my car seat remained lowered) never taking my eyes off the scene. I was locked in and then BAM, there was Salvatore, straying farther than ever before in pursuit of his dog, which continued its roaming ways. I knew I had one chance; the difference between ultimate success and total failure was timing. There were no trains or school buses to blame, nothing to blame but human error, and I was the human. It sounds trite but failure was not an option. Salvatore was closing in on the dog and I suspected his retreat would be swift. I had to move quickly. I sped onto the road as fast as I could without being conspicuous. This was no time to squeal onto the roadway. It was also likely that Salvatore might be more acutely aware of vehicles as his dog neared the road. There was one objective and that was to get between Salvatore and the entrance to the residence. With subpoena and state PI license in hand, I turned into the driveway at a pretty good clip pulling more than halfway in and far enough in to allow me time to stop and hop out of the car before he could get by me. Salvatore had begun his retraction, and was startled as I went past him. I jolted the car into park and popped out of the car when Salvatore was about ten feet from the rear of my car. I was right where I wanted to be. Being within earshot of him and not knowing if he would make a run for his house, I held out the subpoena and firmly stated, "Mr. Tommasso Salvatore you are legally served." He stood frozen and without any expression. As I stepped to him and directed the papers toward his hand I continued, "Failure to appear in court will result in a warrant for your arrest for contempt of court, a class C felony." A few seconds passed as I awaited his verbal or action response. He could have attempted to bolt by me, though I was strategically positioned. If he had, I would have physically forced the papers in his hand and let him drop them. Instead, he calmly looked me up and down and said, "You are standing in a puddle with no shoes." He had broken the ice. I smiled and told him that it was a detail I had overlooked. He took the subpoena from me and without even looking at it said, "Good job," which actually meant a lot to me. I suppose he would rather be served a civil court subpoena by a private investigator than be hunted down by an assassin. I wished him, "Good day," and got in my car. As I backed out of the driveway, I clicked a photograph of Mr. Salvatore, now reading the subpoena, and yes, being followed by his little white dog. In the unlikely event of a denial of service, that one photograph would certainly eliminate any doubt.

As I drove off, my heart still pounding and feeling ecstatic to be able to report the successfully completed service, I couldn't keep the smile off my face. Mr. Salvatore didn't bite for the damsel in distress with the flat tire, but the dog, which I seemed to sense would become a factor when I did the case intake, sure did bite for the trail of beef bouillon I had dribbled down the driveway that morning at four o'clock.

* * *

CHAPTER 10

B4U DATE...INVESTIGATE

Bonus time is what I would refer to on the days when I am hired for the day, at my daily rate, to attend a trial and then to my pleasant surprise, court recesses early. It is not uncommon to be retained to be available during a trial, either as a consultant, a potential witness to impeach the testimony of another witness, or just to be ready to conduct some eleventh-hour investigation work. A single incident of discrediting a piece of testimony of a key witness or casting doubt on an individual's credibility could be enough to sway a jury as to their final disposition in a case. Many cases come down to he said/she said, so credibility is oftentimes what it all boils down to. So when the stakes are high, as they usually are, it proves to be a damn good investment and strategy to have a private investigator available on standby. If a witness, whose testimony is key to a desired verdict, testifies as to A, B, C, and D, and I can go out into the field and refute or even cast doubt on item D alone, the remainder of that individual's testimony is greatly diluted, if not reduced to valueless.

In a criminal trial, where the burden of proof has to be beyond a reasonable doubt, the slightest swaying of a jury will effectuate a not guilty verdict. Also, keep in mind that a jury's verdict in a criminal matter has to be unanimous for a guilty verdict so all you need is an element of doubt in one juror to have the prosecution fall short of their desired guilty verdict.

In a civil matter, the verdict is based upon a preponderance of the evidence; simply put, "more likely than not." A 51 percent likelihood will result in a finding for that position. The best or at least the most familiar example of these criteria is the O. J. Simpson double murder trials. Although the prosecution fell short of convincing a jury that O. J. was guilty beyond a reasonable doubt, the verdict certainly did not equate to "he didn't do it." An ensuing civil trial resulted in a judgment for the plaintiff and against O. J., which technically translated into the fact that the jury felt it was more likely than not that he did, in fact, cause the deaths of Ron Goldman and Nicole Brown Simpson. The verdict did not prove that he committed the act; however, the jury concluded after hearing all of the evidence presented that it was at least 51 percent convinced that he was responsible for the deaths of Nicole Brown Simpson and Ron Goldman.

* * *

I received a very memorable telephone call on one of those bonus days when the judge dismissed us all for the day at 2:00 p.m. My assistant, Sheryl, took the call and passed it on to me. My temptation not to be available—as I wasn't even supposed to be in the office on this day—was overridden by Sheryl's conveyance that a professional-sounding woman had asked to speak with "Mr. Smaha." A quick glance of the pile of case files needing to be dictated, reported, billed, and so on and then my curiosity got the best of me..."I'll take the call." After thanking me for taking the call (like she knew...I have always been leery of women's intuition!), and explaining that a local prestigious law firm had referred her to me, Phyllis articulated a strong need to meet with me. Although it was not absolute, the need and desire to meet in person typically resulted in a serious "real" matter. There was no trepidation of exposing identity or basically pussyfooting around. We were face-to-face thirty minutes later in a rear booth of a local restaurant.

Dr. Phyllis Mellany was a caretaker. Growing up as the oldest of five children, helping with her siblings was expected and it became a way of life. Her medical school years involved intense studying, at which she excelled, but left very little time for "Phyllis."

At the age of twenty-seven, while working as an intern at a large urban metropolitan hospital, Phyllis fell in love with and eventually married Dr. Chad—who else but a fellow intern with whom she had spent eighty hours a week caring for patients? Raising two children and maintaining a medical career made the years slip by quickly. While two medical incomes made the finances secure, it left the marriage anything but. Nurse Nancy moved into the picture and Dr. Chad moved out of Phyllis's life.

After dedicating herself to her profession for over two decades, and finishing raising the two children, now off to Ivy League schools, Phyllis reached a point where she decided that it would be nice to have a social life. She had a lot to offer in that she was bright, personable, attractive, fit, and unattached. At fifty-two, she appeared to be in her early forties. Friends had tried for years to fix her up on blind dates; however, that did not appeal to her, nor did the idea of a dating service.

For years, Phyllis had been reading (for amusement only) the personal ads, but could she ever? No way! Then one day, while surfing the television, she came upon a talk show of couples that met through the personal ads. Phyllis found herself glued to the show. Those very normal-appearing people seemed a lot happier than she was feeling.

The next day, Phyllis found herself once again reading the personal ads, this time with an enhanced level of interest...and amusement. She did not intend to respond, but read the ads with the mind-set of *if I were prone to respond, which one or ones would get my attention?* It was fun and good fantasy in a life of work and stress and, oh yeah, social boredom.

As the days passed, reading the newspaper personal ads became as ritualistic as checking her horoscope. Phyllis monitored the ads and noted how long ads would run. She wondered when an ad stopped running if the placer of the ad had found that someone special. Then one day a new ad jumped out at Phyllis. It read, "DWM, forty-eight, new at this and feeling awkward. Enjoys good communication, fine dining and dancing, laughter and travel—a real catch! This ad placed by his family! Call voice mailbox 4980."

Phyllis took the telephone in her hand. She must have hesitated because the next thing she heard was the operator recording, "If you'd like to make a call...." Why not? Just to hear his voice. It was anonymous. So what if it cost a dollar per minute, money was not an issue. *This is ridiculous,* she thought. What was the big deal in calling anonymously just to listen to a man's voice mail message? Nothing!

William's voice mesmerized her. The message was short, sweet, and sincere, simple but to the point. He articulated so well; his message was *real* sounding, not rehearsed. He had a deep voice of confidence, yet touched with a tone and demeanor of down to earth. Phyllis's mind raced with schoolgirl excitement blended with curiosity and wonderment. Her telephone bill would later reveal that she had called to listen to the recorded massage four times before, you guessed it, writing down William's telephone number.

Phyllis carried William's telephone number with her like a sacred note. She found herself wondering about William in the morning when she awoke, at noon while she ate her lunch (alone), and at night as she tried to slow her rigorous daily pace into rest. William's ad simply invited the caller to continue their response and to call his number. "Let's talk."

The desire to avert the nagging social boredom prevailed and Phyllis punched in the number. RING...eternity...RING...eternity...RING (*Maybe I'll get the answering machine,* she thought and hoped)...Ring...answering machine! "Hi, this is William, sorry I missed your call—" Then suddenly, the phone was picked up—a live voice! Phyllis was so glad that she did not follow her first instinct, which was just to hang up. William was so easy to talk to and made her feel very comfortable. They shared some friendly light conversation; in fact, a lot of friendly conversation. Phyllis could not believe how the time flew, but that initial conversation lasted nearly an hour, an hour that felt like a moment. Her uneasiness and concern about what she should say overshadowed her recollection of the many different topics they discussed. She thought that she must have done all right because the call ended with William asking her if she had been to the new French restaurant downtown called Pierre's.

Their date at Pierre's was nothing less than splendid. William was so polite, so charming, such a gentleman. He made Phyllis feel so special by giving her his undivided attention. He was so interesting too, having traveled all over the world. His stories were fascinating. He seemed too good to be true...but it was true! She knew she wasn't dreaming because she had pinched herself in the ladies' room!

Again, Phyllis figured she must have done all right. At the end of the evening, William walked Phyllis to her front door, took her by the hand, looked straight into her eyes and said, "Phyllis, I've had a wonderful time with you this evening and although you have probably figured out by now that I'm usually not short of words, I am right now. I'd like you to know that I can say with complete certainty that I would love to see you again; however, I do not want to put you on the spot or even begin to make you uncomfortable. Please do not answer me now; however, if you would like to go out again, please call me. My answer is yes...yes. And if I don't hear from you, I wish you the very best, which is exactly what you deserve. You are a wonderful person." William leaned into Phyllis, aimed directly at her cheek, onto which he lightly placed a kiss. "Good night, Phyllis."

"Good night, William, and thank you for a wonderful evening."

As the door closed, Phyllis closed her eyes and froze. She took a deep breath and smiled from ear to ear. A glance at the grandfather clock in her foyer made her wonder if it was too late to call her sister, knowing full well that at 11:20 p.m., her sister had been asleep for hours. Then she thought about her circle of friends. She had to tell somebody. And tell she did; the following day was spent telling and retelling anyone and everyone.

On Monday, Phyllis called William and invited him to dinner at her home for Friday evening. William graciously accepted and asked if he could bring a special bottle of wine he had been saving for a special occasion. A *special bottle...for a special occasion*, she thought. *I think he likes me and it feels so good.*

The week was busy for Phyllis. Besides work, she planned and revised the Friday dinner menu and, of course, called everyone she could think of to quote William's kind words. She arranged to see no patients Friday afternoon to ensure her readiness, and ready she was...two hours early. Her beautiful oceanfront Tudor home was spotless, dinner was prepared, serving was rehearsed, and Phyllis was looking her best thanks to a manicure, facial, and hair trim.

At 7:01 p.m., William turned his car into her well-lit driveway right on time. The evening was once again going splendidly with good communication, comfort, and laughter. He listened to her so intently, and he was such a gentleman, so gracious. He complimented Phyllis more than anyone had in a long, long time—maybe ever. Phyllis kept trying to file away the things he said so she could fill her sister in as soon as he departed. She wanted to tell everyone.

After dinner, Phyllis served William a freshly brewed cup of Chilean coffee. William had mentioned his love of Chile in a previous conversation and she couldn't wait to see if he would recognize her effort. Of course, he did and again made her feel wonderful in appreciation of her consideration.

Architecture was one of William's many interests and he remarked repeatedly of the beauty of Phyllis's home to which a tour was offered. Phyllis guided William through the remainder of the first floor and then to the upper level where William noted the unique roof configuration. As Phyllis was looking up, William moved closer to her, put his hands on her upper arms and kissed her on the lips. Her heart pounded wildly; it felt so good to her. William kissed her again, this time more passionately. Phyllis pulled back a little; William moved forward. Phyllis asked William to stop, but William had other things in mind. He seemed to transform into a different person. William then bullishly moved her into an adjacent bedroom and forcibly raped her.

The horror was indescribable.

When William was done, he departed abruptly, leaving Phyllis sobbing and unable to speak. Without saying a single word, William vanished.

Phyllis didn't know what to do, as a myriad of emotions raged in her head—embarrassment, anger, humiliation, and the thought of her closest friends waiting to hear how the evening went. The damage was irreparable, but the attempt would begin with a telephone call to the police.

Could this horrific nightmare get worse? The answer seemed to be "much worse." The police took a report and Phyllis was asked to go to the hospital for a sexual assault profile examination. It was there that Detective Cheryl Brady explained the cruel reality that this case would probably never get prosecuted. She went on to explain that a jury would have a difficult time agreeing unanimously, beyond a reasonable doubt, with one person's word against another's. Brady told Phyllis that the district attorney liked to win and this case was not a winner.

The DA tried to explain the difficulty of the matter to Phyllis. After all, she had invited him to her home where they drank wine together. They had even gone upstairs and kissed consensually. His version would probably be something to the effect that one thing led to another and when he was finished and didn't say, "I love you," back to her, she flipped out, resulting in a scorned woman rape charge. It was just an unfortunate reality that the criminal justice system could not effectuate true justice in this matter. Phyllis was devastated, victimized, blindsided, and ruined.

Consumed by this woman's passion as she articulated every detail of her story, I could feel her pain. She didn't want sugarcoating or nurturing; she wanted my opinion. She needed to know if there was ANYTHING that could be done. I validated Detective Brady's outlook on the case and threw in a heartfelt slam toward the DA's office along the way. Without the police willing to investigate the criminal aspect of the case because of the DA's reputation for being unwilling to pursue "tough" cases, Phyllis was left with few options. I could conduct a background check on the perpetrator. Although it was a long shot, I might find something. I explained IF this guy had a track record of prior sexual assaults, it would certainly change the way a jury would perceive the alleged events. I emphasized the long shot odds, but explained that it wouldn't be the first time that I handed the DA a guilty verdict on a silver platter. One thing was for certain, if we did not investigate and create a case, no one else was going to do it. In addition, these were all steps that we would need to take if Phyllis was to pursue the matter in a civil proceeding.

The first thing I wanted to find out about this guy was his previous history. If he had a record of sexual assaults, then I believed we had a shot at the criminal arena. Without it, the only possibility of getting into a criminal arena was with a confession, and that was never going to happen, especially because of the second piece I discovered. William was married and had been for the past thirty-two years. He had two grown children and, oh yeah, he wasn't forty-eight, he was fifty-nine! With no more than a couple of hours into this matter, I was feeling that if Phyllis was up for it, there was the potential for a very legitimate civil lawsuit developing. A jury would not like the deception and outright lies. And while in and of themselves, they did not prove rape, it was compelling evidence that would suggest that the sexual assault was possible if not likely. There was more work to be done; however, the preliminary findings were quick, inexpensive, and more importantly, rejuvenating and healing for Phyllis. She had the extreme misfortune to run smack into an evil con artist male bastard. I could see raw emotion and drive generated in her eyes and demeanor as I conveyed to her my findings the next morning over a cup of coffee. She wanted more. She immediately basked in the thought of exposing this man, not only for her own well-being but to possibly prevent him from doing it again. If Phyllis had her way, William was going to pay. She epitomized the "scorned woman" syndrome!

While the events were fresher than they would ever be again, I instructed Phyllis to write down anything and everything she could recall. A detailed account was invaluable in light of the fact that if this was ever going to a trial, it could be a year or more away. A defense lawyer would certainly attempt to challenge her recollection of events from such a long time ago. With this documentation, she could quickly and effectively nip that argument. After securing copies of the advertisements William had placed, I visited the local police department. Even though there was never going to be a criminal proceeding in this matter, the police were required to document their role in the form of an incident report. The fact that Phyllis was in the state of mind to call the police and put herself through the humiliation of a hospital visit to conduct a sexual assault examination would lend credibility to the likelihood that an assault did, in fact, occur. Now it was time for a high-powered attorney.

One of the most common mistakes that people make when in need of legal expertise is to hire an attorney based upon familiarity. The practice of law has become an area of specialty. Just because some attorney helped your sister with her divorce does not equate to him or her being effective in other areas of law. The day of the general practitioner went out with the eight-track music player! There are so many areas in which attorneys specialize. I certainly would not want an attorney who practices primarily in real estate law to defend me in a federal criminal proceeding. They would get eaten up. With that said, I assisted Phyllis in retaining a law firm and lawyer specializing in plaintiff-based civil proceedings. And while I remained on the sidelines at this stage, waiting to assist the attorney as his "in the field" needs emerged, this case was going to boil down to depositions, credibility, and exposure. This case was about legal prowess.

I approached the counter at the Superior Court Civil Division and asked if there were any case files with William as defendant. Within a few minutes, the clerk returned to the window with TWO docket numbers. I asked to view the files, knowing that they were public record. I was told to wait in the viewing room and the files would be brought to me there.

Phyllis was represented by a partner in one of the most prestigious law firms in the area. She brought suit for assault and infliction of emotional distress and demanded over a million dollars in damages. High-powered lawyers retained by William vigorously fought the suit. Expert witnesses testified on both parties' behalf, each concluding after "thorough examination of the evidence and parties in question" that their client was telling the truth and the other was lying. They pretty much washed each other out in terms of effect. The first time I heard Phyllis' story I believed that she was likely not William's first victim. It was my belief all along that there were probably other victims out there who may not have had the resources that Phyllis had access to. Part of my role in this matter was about facilitating publicity via my contacts at the local news stations and newspapers. Once a lawsuit is filed, in this case in superior civil court, it becomes public record. What a story—and I truly believed it, which I conveyed to four different female reporters who rode the white horse to defend their sisterhood...whatever! What I was able to do was convince them to cover the story. Oh, I may have led them all to believe that they were getting to it first; nonetheless, the story got press and even named the defendant in the matter.

In the card game, Fish, you would say...I got what I wanted. I was not playing Fish but I did get what I wanted!

Showing extreme courage and coming forward was Elizabeth Dumont, whose story was frighteningly similar to Phyllis's. William had developed a standard operating procedure using similar props and many, many of the same lines used to lure Phyllis that he used with Elizabeth. It made for very entertaining courtroom drama as the sequestered witness (kept out of the courtroom until they testified), Elizabeth, testified quoting William's same lines used on her as Phyllis had testified to hours earlier. Members of the jury could not always contain themselves, and a few actually let out chuckles as Elizabeth quoted the same sickeningly sweet and obviously insincere words that William had used on her. I think it's safe to say that the jury was not too fond of William and their sentiment was echoed in a verdict in favor of Phyllis, with damages in the two hundred thousand dollar range plus costs and attorney's fees. It pretty much wiped him out financially, which was his half of his marital assets. His wife who promptly divorced his sorry ass got her fair share.

Phyllis was very generous with her settlement. After all, for her it was truly not about the money, though she smiled pretty widely at the verdict. It was about justice, and most importantly, it was about giving William a documented trail. It was her sincere hope that someone else just may be careful and investigate before dating. Her generous contribution to the sexual assault agency would help many victims...as much as healing can be purchased. However, the idea should be that if you are going to expose yourself to the perpetrators that lurk out there, take a measure of precaution and learn how to conduct certain safeguards that may prevent you from being victimized.

* * *

This case deeply affected me. To see a good and decent person victimized provided me with the incentive to attempt to educate whomever possible.

Whether you are about to get involved with someone on a personal level or in a business relationship, you not only have the absolute right but also the obligation to yourself and loved ones to know something about that individual. My vast experience has revealed that being victimized in the personal relationship arena crosses all socioeconomic levels. There is no specificity to race, social class, economic status, or profession. Anyone may become a victim and the hard cold truth of the matter is that if you date, you are a target, and more than likely, you are a vulnerable target.

There is a commonly accepted expression that "knowledge is power." I believe that in this area, but a slight twist to that applies. Knowledge is not only power, but not having the knowledge is nothing less than dangerous. Many people subscribe to the belief that what you don't know won't hurt you. Please don't accept that, because it is my well-founded belief that what you don't know cannot only hurt you, but can also devastate you. Finally, I do not want to make you a skeptic; however, I do want to make you a realist. There are deceitful, evil people out there. You must accept the fact that you are not immune to the possibility of being victimized.

To many people, the idea of investigating someone or 'snooping' into their background conjures up a feeling of discomfort. I suggest you get over it! It may appease those feelings to know that the individual being "checked out" never has to know. Also, the result of a brief inquiry into someone's past may just allow you to progress in a relationship further and with less hesitation. On the other hand, if someone turns out to be far less than you hoped, you may save yourself a lot of pain, suffering, and expense. I have witnessed the devastation and aftermath of various degrees of con artists and, suffice it to say, you are better off if you don't have to become involved with one.

With the technology and information available today via the Internet, conducting a basic check on someone has become very easy. At some point, and at the very least, Google the person. See what that person has for a footprint. Look them up in the phone book. The crude and harsh reality of Phyllis Mellany's tragic episode is that her perpetrator was listed in the local telephone directory as a joint listing...with his wife. Now maybe he would have had a convincing explanation as to that piece of information, but I think it may have started an element of precaution. I always use the analogy that conducting a background investigation on someone is like making a puzzle. No single piece of the puzzle is going to reveal the entire image; however, as the individual pieces of the puzzle (or information) are combined, eventually, a clearer picture is revealed. Those so-called pieces of the puzzle can come from a variety of sources, including first and foremost the Internet. One can also learn a great deal from public record searches like court records. For example, anyone visiting or perhaps telephoning the Superior Court Civil Division where our friend William was found liable to Phyllis could have access to the entire file of that court case. The details found within that file would provide one with enough pieces of the puzzle to reveal quite an image. My experience has shown that once a potential perpetrator suspects that a target is either on to him or her or even smart enough to be skeptical, than he or she moves on quite quickly to the next one.

I have a female friend who, as a matter of standard operating procedure, drops a line in the infancy stages of her getting to know someone that her brother (with whom she is very close) is a detective with the Federal Bureau of Investigation and a third degree black belt! She believes that it helps and that it just may discourage some bastard from abusing her.

The bottom line is this: if you think something bad can't happen to you, then you become even more vulnerable. Taking some degree of precaution will not only reduce your chance of being victimized but also will increase and enhance your ability to move forward in a relationship.

* * *

CHAPTER 11

ISLAND ROMANCE

I got a call from an eighty-two year old gentleman one day, just as I was about to leave the office. Mr. Burnham got right to the point almost as if realizing that at eighty-two you better not procrastinate! He explained that he had been referred to me through his attorney—from a firm I was familiar with and that immediately conjured words like prestigious and old money. He had my interest, yet I had no idea how that would blossom.

Mr. Burnham asked if I had experience at finding people. I quickly assured him I was not able to locate only a few people through the years as an investigator and that unless the individual was in hiding and experienced at it, I would guarantee to locate the person for whom he searched. To nail down the deal, I continued that I was so confident that I could locate the subject of his search that if I were unsuccessful, I wouldn't charge him a dime. He expressed his delight with my response and asked to meet with me as soon as possible, hopefully that evening. I hesitated and glanced at the pile of cases I intended to bill out that evening. In that split-second delay, the tone of Mr. Burnham's voice changed. He echoed an air of need bordering on desperation. "Mr. Smaha, I need your services; time is not on my side." And in case that was not going to do the trick, he threw in there: "I will pay you whatever price you demand when we meet."

We set a meeting time of 6:30 p.m. at a local small chain restaurant. What the hell, I thought, I could always grab a quick dinner and get back to my paperwork later that evening.

Mr. Burnham was a very dapper and physically fit older gentleman, certainly not appearing to be eighty-two. He had a full head of white hair, neatly combed to the side, a tan complexion, and a big warm smile. He was attired in a white golf shirt from some country club, Kelly green pants, and white sneakers that appeared to be worn for the first time. He greeted me with a firm handshake and a simultaneous pat on my shoulder with his left hand, almost as if he wanted to hug me in appreciation for attending to his need. I could not help but be won over by his first impression and imagined that Mr. Burnham must have been a stud in his day. I was already anticipating that he had some illegitimate kid years ago and that he felt a need to find him or her—sort of a cleaning of the slate, if you will, as he approached the twilight of his life. It would not have been the first time for that one.

We sat at a rear booth. After a very brief banter of small talk and Mr. Burnham's profuse thanks for accommodating his need for the meeting, he began. "David, I need to find a woman, a woman I know very little about since we parted over sixty years ago. My wife passed away several months ago after a three-year courageous battle with cancer. She was a wonderful woman and we shared a marvelous life together. Now that she has passed, I have to find a very special person from my past or I will never be able to put it to rest." He took a deep breath and continued, "As a young boy, my family summered on an island off the coast of Maine. Every summer, as soon as school ended, my folks, along with my younger sister and brother and I would pack up the family station wagon and drive for eight hours from upstate New York. We then took the car ferry to Chebeague Island to our final destination, an old cottage overlooking Casco Bay that had been left to my mom when her parents passed away. It was a charming old home, where we spent ten weeks of good old-fashioned summer fun—swimming in the cold Atlantic, jumping from the ferry dock as the ferry pulled away leaving a big foamy wake, days on the beach playing, and evenings around a campfire, laying on the hammock, swinging for hours on the porch swing, and playing with the other kids on the island who, for the most part, were only there for the summer as well.

"There was a girl next door, as they say, and we played together every day as very young children. The gender was irrelevant. We created adventure and spent nearly every waking hour with each other. When one of us arrived at the island for the summer before the other, you could rest assured the first one there would be on the ferry dock to greet every morning and afternoon ferry until the other arrived. Generally, my family got to the island first. I vividly recall seeing her each year. She would be standing on the upper level of the ferry, standing on a bench waving away and smiling ear to ear. As soon as the ferry was tied down, she was the first one off the boat. She would run to see me and I would jump with joy to see her. Without losing a beat, I would pick up her stride and we would run together to our secret fort, which I would have already tidied up in anticipation of her arrival.

"'Just as we left it,' she'd say with a sigh of relief.

"As we grew from early childhood innocence, I recall one year when she arrived, still waving and smiling, but holy cow; she had really grown that year! I believe we were twelve years old. She was all of a sudden taller than me. On this particular year, the little girl running off the ferry had evolved into a casual stride down the ramp and a 'Hey, Don, what's up?'

"With the onset of adolescence, the next few years were a little awkward. We still hung out, but not all the time. I was never quite sure what she was thinking or what would make her happy. She was mysterious and difficult to figure out.

"By the time we were about fourteen, we were back together again but now we were gender sensitive. I was enamored of her smile and her laughter and watching her lips as she spoke. I would try to be discreet as I glanced at her breasts in her swimsuit. For the first time in my life, I was physically and sexually attracted to a girl.

"One night as we were walking back home from a beach bonfire, hearing the surf and walking under the light of a large glowing moon and a sky full of stars, I found the nerve to reach for her hand as we climbed a little incline leading from the beach to the road. Feeling the safety of being able to discount the move, if necessary, as only trying to help her (as if she had ever needed it before), I took her by the hand as she stepped onto the upper level path we had traveled a thousand times. As we continued along, I didn't let go of her hand, nor did she try to pull away. It felt so good. We both smiled as if to give each other non-verbal permission that it was OK. The next thing I knew, we were kissing. I mean really kissing each other. I will never forget it.

"Not that anyone saw us that evening but we must have given off some vibe because from that night on, we almost had to go undercover. Her parents, who had been feuding with my parents over a foolish fence or boundary issue between our properties, had let her know that they did not approve of me. Her family was a lot wealthier and higher class than mine and they were now playing their cards. In a nutshell, I was not good enough for their daughter. So we sneaked around, which in some ways made it even more fun.

"Well, summer fun had to end but as it had in the past, it resumed the next summer. She had grown even more beautiful and had grown in all the right places, if you know what I mean."

I nodded and smiled.

"Well, without getting into all the details, we became very close…very close. We were each other's first if you know what I mean. Looking back, I know we were young, but it was true love.

"I remember so well watching her leave at the end of August that year. She asked me to not be at the ferry dock because, as she put it, it was not worth the hassle her parents would give her all year trying to put down my family and me. By now, the boundary dispute feud had turned ugly and there were overheard conversations about lawyers and legal battles. Looking back, I truly believe that my parents were very much in the right, but her parents thought they were never wrong and were accustomed to getting their way. They had money and lawyers and were able to push people around. They were the big-city slick type and we were more down-to-earth country folk. Anyway, that summer

I sat on the bank and watched the ferry chug away. She knew where I would be watching from and stared until the distance had made us grow so small we vanished. She discreetly blew me a kiss; I blew one back and sat there and sobbed like a baby. I loved her with all my heart and my sixteen-year-old heart ached like it never had before."

As I sat across from this man I had known for less than an hour, I could not help but be grateful to have met him. Even as he told this sixty-plus-year-old story, he did so with such passion. I was feeling the emotion he exuded. With a deep breath to overcome the hurdle of that memorable and difficult episode of his life, he continued.

"The next summer was unbelievable. We reconnected like there had never been any separation. She had a job as a waitress in the evening at the big old inn on the island and I was a lobsterman's helper six days a week, so we made the best of the days off or days when my boss opted to not go out. One night in early August, we got into our first big discussion, which led to the closest thing we had ever come to an argument. I realized that in a few short weeks that she would be off to college, New York University, majoring in fashion and design.

"My fear of losing her probably caused me to act as if I was chasing her away. It was easy to feel as if I was not good enough for her. She had grown into the most gorgeous young woman you could ever imagine. In addition, she was bright and witty; she'd fill a room with her smile and personality. It seemed that everyone who met her was stunned by her qualities. She wanted to be famous and she already looked the part. Who was I except a young man who truly loved her? I wanted what was best for her and I was convinced that she would meet him in college. Her parents would love him and approve of him and they would all live happily ever after.

"As the summer nights turned cool, so did our time together. I learned that she was leaving the island early that year as *college* started before Labor Day. One day shortly before she was going to leave, she was upset because she had received word that by way of a lottery, she did not get on-campus dorm living accommodations. This meant that she would be living at home her freshman year and taking a twenty-minute train ride to campus each day. Although I pretended to empathize with her, secretly I was thrilled. The thought of her living with thousands of similarly aged college students made my fearful imagination spiral out of control.

"I knew this would be our final summer on the island. Her area of study would require her to work in the fashion district of New York City; it was where she always dreamed to work. And my folks had already decided that the feud had grown beyond comfort. They had had enough and were prepping the cottage to be in *sell* condition.

"Our good-bye was set for a Sunday evening. She was scheduled to depart the following afternoon. I had been secretly renovating our childhood fort into as close a replication as possible to the days when we played in there as seven- and eight-year-olds. I wanted so desperately to make our last evening special. I placed candles on a dozen flat surfaces, tacked photos of our childhood fun on the walls and even wrote her a poem.

"I hated this good-bye. I knew somehow I'd get through it, but I feared the future. The thought of life without her was unbearable.

"I met her as planned and we hugged. Then we held hands and walked without saying much. I pretended to have no particular direction in mind. As we strolled along the dirt road and neared the area of our old fort, she brought it up. Without letting on, I played it off and continued to walk in that direction. I couldn't wait to be there. I wanted to see her face. I wanted to stay there forever.

"It was getting dark as I ducked into the fort. I got ahead of her and was able to light several candles as she entered my new pad. She stood at the entrance and sobbed. Just the reaction I was looking for!

"That night was very special. We cried but we also laughed. We exchanged 'I love you' over and over as we held each other like there was no tomorrow. We talked seriously. I told her that I did not want to get in the way of her college or her fun or her bright future. She told me that I never would or could and that made me feel a little better. We agreed to give each other a month and if we still felt the same, then we could write and maybe we could arrange a visit. All of a sudden, I realized that her living on campus would have worked out much better, but it was no time to sweat the details. She handed me a piece of paper on which she had written her address and, 'Donald, I will always love you. Please write; I'll write right back, I promise.'

"The thirty days gave me plenty of time to write a masterpiece. I was in my senior year of high school so I had a lot of free time. I would get my schoolwork done, finish my chores, and lock myself in my bedroom every night. I probably crumpled up hundreds of pieces of paper trying to compose the perfect letter. Finally, day twenty-seven and my work was complete. I dropped the letter into the mailbox, jiggled the handle to ensure its safety, and said a quick prayer that the letter would do the trick.

"I waited and waited and waited but never got a response. After three painful weeks of running to our mailbox, I could not stand it any longer so I wrote her again. Again, I received no response. She could not bear to tell me, I thought, so loving her the way I did, I backed off. It was years before the pain subsided, but eventually, life went on. I married a girl I met through work, raised three children, and was blessed with seven grandchildren.

"Then one day about ten years ago I was in Boston with my wife walking down Boylston Street. Approaching from the opposite direction, there she was. I knew her look and beauty instantaneously. We both stopped in our tracks. Her eyes met mine. The look on her face, and likely mine, expressed volumes.

"'Don, is that really you? You look marvelous; how have you been?' as we extended our arms to hug. I closed my eyes and for an ever so brief moment, I felt as if I was a teenager and we were in our fort. Wake me up, I thought. The only words I could form were, 'Emily, I can't believe that it's you.' Frozen in the moment, we both seemed to catch ourselves and proceeded to introduce our respective spouses. Emily took control of the situation, as she was always able to do and explained that we were childhood friends and had not seen each other for fifty years. My first reaction was to clarify and modify the word 'friend' but realized that no good would come of it. After a few brief exchanges of how many children and grandchildren we each had and where we settled down, my wife and her husband seemed to engage in a courtesy discourse to allow Emily and me a few moments. It was surreal. We let each other know how great each other looked and that our lives had been happy. And then I discreetly told her that I always loved her and never forgot her. I softened my voice and let her know how difficult it was for me to get over her, at which point she interrupted me and asked, 'Then why didn't you ever write to me; I waited to hear from you but you never wrote.' I felt like I had just watched the ferry depart from the island. 'Oh, Emily, I wrote to you more than once but you never responded so I let you go. I figured that was what you wanted.' Emily reached for my hand and squeezed it. 'Oh, Don…oh my Lord. I didn't think you wanted to deal with my family and me. God rest his soul, my father must have intercepted your letters. Oh my good Lord, I am so, so sorry.' I could see her eyes welling up with tears.

"The entire world stopped. The whirlwind of devastation I felt at that moment was immeasurable, like nothing I had ever experienced in my lifetime. What could have been, but could no longer. After only a few more moments, we parted ways, both stunned and saddened though not wanting to reveal it for a number of very good reasons. It was likely apparent, as I recall my wife asking me if I was all right. I was not.

"As you can imagine, this has haunted me and this is where I need your help. I want to locate Emily. I need to answer my *what if?* I can't help but wonder what if her husband passed away. Could we share whatever time we have left. I still felt magic when I saw her ten years ago. I feel our love endured the years. I need so badly to find her, can you help, David?"

I was so consumed by this man and his story. And now, I was going to become part of this epic tale of long lost love. "Mr. Burnham, I will find Emily; let's not let another moment be wasted; let's get to work."

For the next half hour, I took control of the conversation and drilled my new client with more questions than anyone could ever conceive based on the limited current information. Of greatest significance, Mr. Burnham recalled from their brief encounter that Emily had spoken about having a newspaper column and that she and her husband resided just outside Los Angeles. They were only in Boston for her husband's college class reunion. I peppered him with questions and extracted every detail he may never have realized he knew, including information about the location of the island property. There was always the possibility that Emily's property was still owned by a family member. I always enjoyed this part of fact-finding. After a client would say, "That's about all I know," I would proceed to prove the client wrong. I felt it was my job to exhibit that expertise and justify the client's need for my services.

I felt I had enough and wanted to get on this quickly. As I drove back to my office, I was already having thoughts of this reuniting love story being *Oprah* worthy! I could only imagine these two childhood sweethearts denied a life together by a deceased, controlling, mail-filtering father and then finding each other with their love sustained over a lifetime.

Less than two hours later, I had located a telephone listing for our girl, one Emily Dow-Lancaster, Mulholland Drive, Los Angeles, California. It was not uncommon for wealthy women not to want to vacate their original names. She had kept her name to a degree by hyphenating it with her husband's name. I took advantage of the three-hour time difference, telephoned the *L.A. Times* and eventually got to a person with whom I pleaded for help. She was able to identify Emily for me as having had a column in the Society section of the paper "years ago." From there, it was as easy as directory assistance!

Normally, I would sit on this information for at least a day.

In this case, I telephoned Mr. Burnham immediately. He answered the telephone on the first half ring. I imagined him sitting in a recliner with his hand readied for my call. I told him that I believed I had located Emily and that I had her address and a corresponding telephone number. "It's three hours earlier in California. Do you want to call her?"

He did not hesitate in his response, "No, no, would you call her, David? I don't want to interfere in any way if she is married. I would only want to speak with her if by chance her husband has passed."

"Stand by, Mr. Burnham"

Typically, I never hesitated to make a call. Having a rough idea as to how I would start a dialogue usually led to the rest of the words flowing smoothly. My belief was that prepared dialogue was very restrictive and didn't sound right. Rehearsed words just didn't flow and didn't effectuate the desired result compared to winging it. This time was a little different. Although I felt no need to rehearse a script as if I was selling phone service, I took a few moments to think about how I would approach this woman. I think the difference this time was the emotional involvement I was feeling. I was not supposed to allow myself to get emotionally involved but if I hadn't, I would have been nothing more than a machine. In hindsight, there was no way I could have prepared for what I was about to hear.

An older female voice answered, "Hello."

"Good evening, is this Emily?"

After a slight hesitation, "Who is calling, please?"

"My name is David Smaha. Is this Emily?"

"No, this is her daughter. Can you please tell me what this is in reference to?"

"Of course, again, my name is David Smaha. I'm a private investigator and I've been asked to locate Emily for an old friend of hers, Donald Burnham. Is she available?"

I was clearly at the mercy of Emily's daughter. She was in charge here and I could not risk being evasive or offending her. The thought of not getting through and having to report to the eagerly awaiting Mr. Burnham, who was, in my mind, sitting with his hand on the telephone, was far beyond what I wanted to jeopardize. It was time to open up and lay it out. There was nothing to lose and everything to gain. My experience was that people generally respond favorably to the vulnerability of spilling one's guts, so I proceeded to do just that.

"Oh, David…this is so sad. My mother passed away three weeks ago. She had been widowed for nearly seven years, so I cared for her as she failed and was with her every day. Mom told me all about

Donald. She loved him every day of her life and was so deeply saddened to think about what had happened and what was never to be. He was her first love and she always remembered him through her long and eventful life."

I explained that Donald's wife had passed away as well and that he could not stop thinking about Emily.

The daughter continued, "How sweet that he sought her out after all those years. Did you know about their chance meeting in Boston ten years ago?"

"Yes, and they were both with their spouses. Donald did not want to pursue any contact if your mom was still with your father but since his wife had passed, he had to find out."

"My mom told me that she actually did something similar after my dad died but determined that Donald was still married. She opted not to call him though she wanted to talk with him so badly."

After a few more exchanges, Emily's daughter, Mary, asked me if I would pass along her telephone number to Donald, should he ever want to talk. She let me know that she would love to talk with him about a woman they both dearly loved, but only if he would be comfortable doing so. With sadness, we said our good-byes.

This next call was never going to get easier so I didn't hesitate. Once again, Mr. Burnham answered right away. I had only known him for about five hours yet I could feel his pain as he digested the news. He seemed pleased to know that before she passed away, Emily had shared their story with her daughter. He declined to take Mary's number. He simply wanted to be alone with his thoughts and memories.

Two days later, I received a call from Mr. Burnham, who sounded strong and resolved to go on. He wanted Mary's telephone number, which I had ready in case he changed his mind. He wanted to hear about what she had shared with her daughter about him, about them. I believed he was looking for closure on an upbeat and I know he found it.

A few weeks later I received a check and a shakily handwritten note. I saved it—not the check, the note! I read it from time to time. Although it never came to be, I like to imagine the life these two people could have shared if not for the meddling parent.

In the note, Donald told me that he and Mary had spoken on the phone several times and that she had flown to the East Coast to meet and visit with him. She brought with her several scrapbooks of photos from her mother's lifetime. Mary and Donald took a ride on the island ferry and a walk on the island where Donald and Mary's mother first met, played, and fell in love. Mary loved seeing where her mother grew up. She wanted to meet the man her mother first fell in love with. Together, they both laughed and cried just as Donald had with Emily over sixty years ago. They both wanted to, and were able to—as he so eloquently described in his note to me—celebrate her life.

CHAPTER 12

DOUBLE MURDER-DOUBLE JEOPARDY-DOUBLE TROUBLE

I was departing the County Superior Court with a prominent defense attorney on a very cool and crisp autumn day when he suddenly stopped to acknowledge the season. He commented that you could almost feel it in the air, the change of season. I responded along the lines that we were fortunate that we both were avid skiers, which made the winter tolerable at worst and even enjoyable for a time. With a clever smile revealing his amusement that I had taken his bait, he told me that he wasn't referring to the next season as winter but instead, "murder season." It was his experience—and irrefutably substantiated by the statistics—that many of the relatively low number of murders in the state occurred during the cold winter months. When you combine the facts that so many murders are domestic related and the stress of the holidays and the bitter cold weather conditions lead to a well-known affliction known as "cabin fever," it really does make perfect sense.

As if he had had a premonition, I received a telephone call from that same attorney a couple of weeks later, the day after Thanksgiving. There had been a double murder in a small rural town called Treadmont. So much for a nice long weekend! I prided myself on being assessable; I was in my car driving to the scene within twenty minutes.

The details were sketchy and vague. What else could be expected at this point? The facts provided were that two young adult males were dead, shot in the head at very close range while lying on couches at a hunting camp. Two male suspects had been taken into custody and there was one potential female witness who was allegedly in the hunting camp when the men were murdered.

As I drove north, I reminded myself of my duty and responsibility. I was working on a court authorization with state taxpayer dollars. My ultimate goal was to determine what exactly happened, what was the truth of the matter. All I had at this stage were questions but I felt confident, as I always did, that I would eventually get them answered. I had no idea the direction that would lead to the answers and that is why I loved my job!

The murder scene was a dilapidated one-and-a-half-story shack-style wooden structure used annually during the months of September and October to house migrant apple pickers. The name of the rural road on which it was located was Macintosh Lane, as the vast area was heavily populated with apple trees. Apparently, the men had taken possession of the property in early November to not only reside in but also to get in some good hunting. Even I could connect the dots that the area must provide a prime hunting environment although there may have been a slight misunderstanding as to what the men were hunting for.

By the time I was at the crime scene, the State Police had already processed it. And though I knew that anything like blood samples or DNA or important physical evidence had been documented and catalogued, it was now in the hands of the crime lab. It was my experience that this area of investigation, often referred to as forensics, was not the arena most likely to reveal discrepancy, impropriety, or incompetence. Not that it could not occur, as another case story will reveal; however, the reality was that it was largely out of my control and technically, over my head. My belief foundation was that if an impropriety did occur, then there would be an abundance of clues suggesting it within the human behavior surrounding the police investigation.

I was accompanied at the crime scene by a couple of State Police homicide detectives who made no attempt whatsoever to hide their feeling of being inconvenienced by what they felt was unnecessary, namely me! One of the detectives, Detective Thomas, who I would determine to be the lead detective on the case, was very young. I had never seen him or heard his name before. I decided that my game with these guys was to play out the same shit they were dealing—inconvenienced.

I thought to myself that this was going to be like gravy on their turkey. "Can't these scumbags ever commit their crimes during the week? I've got family visiting from all over the country and hot turkey sandwiches waiting for me at home." They seemed to like it. I was there because I had to be there, not to be a hero or contentious or to question their supreme authority and ability.

The way I had it figured, Detective Thomas was living proof of the Peter Principle. Two months earlier, he was probably aiming his radar gun at speeding motor vehicles on the interstate. I could just imagine him getting out of his blinking blue cruiser, adjusting his big brimmed hat, and strutting to the driver's window of a pulled-over vehicle. He had been so good at what he did; he was promoted to sergeant of the Traffic Division. When it was time for his next promotion, he landed a position as a detective...do you see the logic? Neither did I, though I had seen it play out time and time again, especially in law enforcement.

As I canvassed the scene, Detective Thomas let out a goofy comment of relief, "Don't think there's much mystery here; everyone says it was Brent who did it."

Continuing my "Mickey the Dope" routine but finding him irresistible, I asked him to help me out. "There were five people here; Kenny and Peter are dead; Brent and Robert, who are half brothers, are both being held on murder charges; and the only possible witness, a teenage girl named Samantha is Robert's girlfriend and mother of his child, oh yeah, and pregnant again."

"Define 'everyone,' detective."

"Everyone is everyone I've spoken with likes Robert and hates Brent. Everyone says that it has to be Brent because they knew he could do something like this and they don't believe that Robert was the type to kill people. It's pretty much case closed."

I could not believe what I was hearing. "What's the motive, detective?"

"Don't know, don't really matter," he replied.

I repeated his words slowly as if trying hard to understand some hidden meaning to his response, "Don't know, don't really matter." I decided that the right thing to do was to shut my mouth and let it play out on the field, which in this case was the courtroom.

I continued doing my thing, which was taking photos and measurements and pensively walking around the place. Every now and then, I'd stop and take down some notes. Then I said, "Well, that should do it for now. It was nice to meet you. I'm sure we'll be talking again, Detective Thompson." I wanted to see if he'd correct me.

"It's 'Thomas,'" he said.

"Oh thanks, it was nice to meet you, Thomas. I'll let you know when I figure out the motive. It is simply amazing to me that you solved this double murder without ever having determined the motive." Before he could conjure up a response in his big fat head, I departed. Knowing it would end up personal and ugly between us, I wanted to waste no time in making it personal. I took a small degree of pleasure in making him hate me. The more he hated me, the more I got him off his game, if he even had one, I thought.

This guy was the biggest turkey I had ever encountered in police work. I wanted to say so many things like, "You must be relieved to have survived another Thanksgiving." I was saving another line I had reserved for him, "Is this your full-time job or are you just doing this for some extra Christmas shopping money?" I cannot say that at the time I knew what I was doing although instinctively, it just felt right.

As the evidence in the case poured in, the unknowns became increasingly fewer. No one questioned or disputed that a double murder had occurred. There had been, in fact, five individuals in a seven-hundred-square-foot one-and-a-half-story shack/camp. Kenny and Peter were both shot in the head from close range. The victims had been asleep on two separate couches in the living room. Kenny was on the black couch and was most likely shot first, as forensics determined that the gun was fired less than an inch from his head. The first shot likely startled Peter who had been asleep on the white couch as his head wound was delivered at close range as he was lifting his head. Samantha, whose versions varied depending upon who was asking and how the questions were phrased, was consistent on some things. She had been upstairs at the time of the shootings and recalls that the shots were a few seconds apart. After the shots were fired, she peeked through a crack in the top of the stairs. She did not witness the actual shootings. By the time she looked, she saw Kenny and Peter lying dead on the couches with blood all over the place, especially around their heads.

Robert and Brent were half brothers, sharing the same mother, different fathers. Brent was the older brother at twenty-nine and Robert was known to have always looked up to him despite or maybe because of Brent's run-ins with the law. In their world, your record was your badge of honor, a status symbol of sorts. Many facts were also emerging from the individual suspects as well as Samantha that people were agreeing were consistent. Brent and Robert had been out hunting early the morning of the murders. They returned together at approximately 9:00 a.m., at which time Samantha, having heard the door upon their entry, began to descend the rickety wooden steps. She was told to go back upstairs, by whom would later become a critical piece of testimony. Without questioning whoever sent her back upstairs, she returned and perked her ears as to what may be happening. She recalled that she sensed trouble. Here is where her story flip-flopped. In most of her interviews, Samantha stated that she had no recollection of hearing anything prior to the shots, which occurred a minute or two after she returned upstairs. She provided a variety of versions of things she heard immediately following the gunshots. This would turn out to be what this case would hinge upon since there was no motive—at least according to the lead detective for the state.

The facts were also very consistent surrounding the events from shortly after the time of the shooting until the two men were taken into custody. There was no denying that both men had taken part in the cleanup and attempted cover up, pathetic as it was. The disposal of the bodies and the bloodied couch cushions consisted of simply throwing them a few feet into the woods off the road about a half-mile from the murder scene. What made the move especially ineffective was that it was in the middle of hunting season.

There would be no doubt, none whatsoever, that one of these two men had committed a heinous and cowardly double murder. And although the other one participated in an unprepared attempt to cover up the crime for his half brother, he had not committed an act punishable by life in prison. The question that I was trying to comprehend was not *who had the capacity*, because I believe that provoked, almost anyone can get into a state of mind to pull a trigger, but what would motivate someone to commit murder? Most killers talk about some hard-to-explain mind-set where they temporarily lose control of all reason and judgment. To me, and apparently only to me at this point, this case was about what would motivate either one of them to kill these two men as they lay asleep on a couch. This was not a random act. Something provoked this double murder and I was determined to understand what that motive was.

As a court-appointed private investigator authorized upon the request of Brent's attorney, I was technically afforded access to visit with him at the county jail. Although the time would come when I would want to make that connection, I never liked going into that arena without first attaining some information. To speak with a defendant at that early stage was potentially not fruitful. I preferred to get some information so that I could better determine his or her credibility. To go in early, I would just be going to be able to listen and throw out uninformed general questions. Whether the person was guilty or not, nine times out of ten I would hear the same thing, "I didn't do it." In reality, nine times out of ten, they did do it. It was that one in ten, that falsely charged defendant, that made my heart pound and my blood boil. There were many occasions when that erroneous charge was a true mistake. There were others where it was a matter of misguided incompetence. And there was always the possibility, as I had seen before, that malicious and sick members of the law enforcement society acted in a manner of knowing and intentional injustice. Back to this double murder.

The bottom line on the one potential key witness, Samantha, was that she didn't really know who had shot Kenny and Peter. Her version of events the morning of the shooting were inconsistent and only served to solidify the fact that she had no idea what occurred after she was sent back upstairs when Brent and Robert returned from their early morning hunting.

Whatever triggered these murders had occurred prior to that morning, unless they were shot for snoring…kidding.

Robert was similarly aged to the victims and had been known to hang out with them. Robert was consistently characterized as good friends with Kenny, although like any friends, they had been known to argue. Peter was more Kenny's friend and was only visiting for a few days. Brent had just returned to the area after serving two years in a Massachusetts prison for burglary. The local police had been very relieved to learn of his little sabbatical away from the area and equally disappointed that he was back. They had arrested him a dozen times from the time he was fourteen until he took his show on the road and was incarcerated in Massachusetts.

Neither suspect was talking to the police on the advice of their respective attorneys. In the many hours prior to the suspects being represented, they miraculously managed to keep their mouths shut, despite the clever tactics by the lead detective.

"So Robert, you don't want to say nothing; that's fine, because we're getting an earful from

Brent. He says you did it. If you want to take the rap for him and spend the rest of your life behind bars, you're quite a brother. But if you want me to help you, that's what I'm here to do. You want me to help you or not?"

Robert just stared at him without uttering a word.

The police concluded from that exchange or lack thereof that Robert was either scared of Brent or had been coached already, or likely both of those things. They didn't seem to consider that maybe Robert HAD killed Kenny and Peter and wasn't going to say his innocent brother had done something when he hadn't.

The investigation was conducted by a variety of different detectives, all under the direction of the lead detective, Thomas. In the criminal justice system, a prosecutor depends nearly entirely upon the evidence presented by the police investigation. When you think of it, the detective on the front line wields an incredible amount of power and influence. In this matter, as is very often the situation, a cop decides who committed a crime and then seeks out the evidence to substantiate the theory. It is only natural and understandable (I didn't say right) that as he or she comes upon physical evidence or even testimony that refutes the theory, he or she may ignore it. Thus, the prosecutor never really has the complete picture and, ultimately, justice is compromised.

In this matter, it resulted in a travesty of justice.

After Thomas decided that it had to be Brent who committed the crime, his strategy became transparent. He would ignore any incriminating evidence toward Robert, turn a deaf ear to testimony pointing toward Robert, and leave the prosecutor in the dark. With very little to go on, the prosecutor made a strategic decision; in fact, based upon what he had to go on, he made a brilliant decision. It was obvious that one of the men had committed the crime. If a jury knew that one of the men was not guilty, then it could only follow that the other one WAS guilty. So the state would push for Robert's trial first and although pretend to prosecute, the state realized it had a very weak case. What they didn't realize is that there was a very strong case out there; however, in my opinion, the detectives made a knowing and conscious choice to disregard very pertinent evidence and testimony. After the state lost Robert's case, then they could proceed with Brent's trial with only one possible alternative remaining. A logical approach but riddled with one slight glitch in their way...the truth.

I believed Brent when he told me that he had not done this. But when Robert was found not guilty, all fingers pointed toward Brent. In order to find Brent not guilty, I had to find a reason why Robert would have wanted to murder these two guys. I had to find a motive and I didn't have to look very far.

If I have learned anything through the years, it is that people love to talk. They want to tell you what they know. And although I have no formal psychology training, I have a theory. If someone knows something and never tells anyone, then they have no validation for knowing whatever it is. People seem to feel empowered by "knowing." It might suggest that they are "in." Think about the way someone lets you know that he or she knows. It is done with pride. "I know" or "I knew that already" or better yet, "I know something you don't know." In a nutshell, my job as an investigator is to let the interviewee know that it is OK to let me know what he or she knows.

In this matter, it was getting to spend time with the family of the two suspects. I would sit in the single-wide trailer hour after hour, chatting with the group, and then one by one, isolate a member and let him or her know that I knew that he or she knew more than the others. It was like taking candy from a baby. The younger brother wanted so much to be in the know, to prove that he actually hung out with his older brothers. Of course, the trap or the danger is that you could be lied to in order to impress. Nothing was absolute or even credible until heard, confirmed, and then confirmed again.

Younger brother Toby had a theory based upon what he knew, and it was pretty good. Toby revealed that the only thing that ever pissed off his brother Robert was when someone flirted with his girl. "You see, Robert's girl, Samantha, was not all there," Toby explained. I had firsthand knowledge of that little piece of information. "So when guys flirted with her, she liked it and flirted back." This drove Robert completely crazy. He had a violent and explosive temper that would emerge when he witnessed or learned of anyone flirting with his girl.

The problem was that his girl, in the lowest common denominator of human behavior, enjoyed the attention right down to the core. Not only did the attention she received make her feel good, when her man got insanely jealous, that behavior validated his love for her. In her very simple psychology, it worked for her.

Now the evidence.

Within the police reports obtained through the discovery process, which allowed both sides to have access to witness statements, the pieces of the puzzle began to fit together. Samantha made several lengthy statements and responded to hours of interrogation, which resulted in hundreds of pages of reports. Several times, she made mention that Robert and Brent had been taking off and disappearing for many hours at a time. They never told her where they were going, but she suspected that they were up to no good!

Samantha stated repeatedly that Robert was very jealous.

Samantha also stated that she and Robert fought over his frequent and lengthy absences and she made it clear that she didn't like it. Robert responded that he had no choice.

Samantha told the detectives within her statements that she told Robert, "Don't be dazzlin' me," and then he got extremely upset. There was no further elaboration on the comment.

When I asked Samantha what that meant, she explained that "dazzlin'" was when a guy leaves his girl alone with other men and doesn't care what happens in terms of those men hitting on her, almost like offering her up. Samantha admitted to me that she was telling Robert stories about one of the men, Kenny, in order to make Robert jealous. She told him that he was hitting on her, especially when they were all drinking late at night...while Robert and Brent were out and about.

I told her she was clever, and she smiled with pride. Samantha wasn't as dumb as everyone thought. She'd get her man nice and jealous and that would make him stay home. Robert may love doing things with his older brother, but she knew his hot button.

Knowing that in a courtroom I would be repri-manded for leading the witness, I enjoyed my free-dom and asked the young lady, "Samantha, what's the most jealous thing that Robert has ever said or done?" (In other words, prove to me the ingredi-ents of your brilliant plan.)

I couldn't help but think I was coming down the homestretch when she replied.

"Well, last summer he told John Dumont that he'd kill him if he ever flirted with me again and then three hours later, he fired a gun at his feet 'cause he was talking to me at the bonfire." Robert then threatened Dumont that the next shot would be in his head if he ever flirted with his girl again.

As many times as I scrutinized the reports, there was no mention of this within the police reports, despite the fact that Samantha told me with certainty that she had told the cops the same information. The motive was clear to me.

I located Mr. Dumont who confirmed the incidents Samantha had conveyed to me. Dumont described Robert as crazy, and in his opinion, capable of murder. In fact, there was no doubt in Dumont's mind that Robert had killed the men, and he knew why it happened. He said the minute he heard about the murders, he (and his other friends) knew.

What I found most disturbing is that the police had interviewed Mr. Dumont and he told them everything he told me.

I don't believe the prosecutor ever knew about this information. If he did, why would he not bring it up during Robert's murder trial? In the words of a well-known court watcher, the prosecutor looked defeated from the opening argument to his lack of cross-examination of the defendant (who took the stand and faced no difficult questioning) to closing statements. It was no surprise that the jury returned a verdict of not guilty in a very short fifty-two minutes of deliberations.

Three months later, older brother Brent's trial began. The state aggressively drove home all the grisly details of the murder and the jury was convinced that the double murder was perpetrated by one of the two men. Robert testified for the state and the jury was able to figure that he had already been tried and that he was a free man. The only detail the state had to overcome was the defense's prosecution of Robert.

One by one, witnesses testified of Robert's volatility and rage when associated with Samantha being flirted with. Not only did Brent's jury acquit him in a very short time, but the jurors with whom I spoke all told me that they would have found Robert guilty had that been their directive to determine.

I know that what occurred in this matter was criminal but, I believe, in two very different and distinct ways.

* * *

A terrible and heinous crime was committed that Thanksgiving morning on a back road in a small northern town. It was an unplanned (or at least not well planned), emotionally charged act of jealous rage. In the words of the defendant, Kenny was the target and Peter was in the wrong place at the wrong time. A man with a gun in his hands pulled the trigger. He knowingly and intentionally deprived two young men the opportunity to live their lives—murder.

There was another terrible and heinous crime committed in this matter, in the wake of the double murder. An inexperienced, incompetent lead homicide detective rushed to judgment and completely botched the investigation. Instead of actually doing his job, which was to investigate and gather all the evidence leading to a logical conclusion, he reached an unsubstantiated and unfounded conclusion first. He did so without even considering a motive. As a result, his "investigation" and the gathering of evidence were guided by a desire to substantiate and achieve his ill-founded conclusion. In doing so, the most important evidence in the case was ignored and omitted…because it refuted his premature determination. Law enforcement officials who had taken an oath ignored convincing and credible evidence because it did not support the result for which they were striving.

A horrific tragedy was averted by the superior court judge authorizing funding for a private investigation to be conducted, independent of the state and police investigation. Had that not occurred, it is highly likely that an innocent man would have been convicted of a double murder he did not commit and likely been sentenced to either a very lengthy period of incarceration to life in prison with no chance of parole.

This near travesty should scare the shit out of us as a civil society—our trusted law enforcement officials have the capacity and discretionary power to take the lives of innocent people. The definition of murder includes the language "knowingly and intentionally taking the life of another human being." I submit that a sixty- to eighty-year prison sentence effectuates the taking away of someone's life. In this matter, it resulted in what I will refer to as attempted murder. The reality is that many times the attempt comes to fruition and the innocent party is framed. It doesn't just happen in highlighted stories on prime time shows like *Dateline* or *48 Hours*. It happens every day in small towns all across this country. It occurs in the small towns where our school-aged children daily recite the Pledge of Allegiance professing, "with liberty and justice for all."

In a travesty of justice, the guilty party did not and will never pay the price for taking the lives of two innocent victims.

I will always be saddened, especially for the families of the victims, that the guilty party will never be held accountable. I am also saddened by the fact that the law enforcement official(s) who committed the atrocity will never be exposed or held accountable. My experience suggests that their getting away with what they did or didn't do will only support and encourage them to perpetuate their twisted, sick, and criminal vision upon our criminal justice system again.

* * *

CHAPTER 13

DRAMA CAMP ROI

Subpoena Service. It sounds so simple—hand deliver this one or these two pieces of paper into the hand of another individual.

The subject's name was Dan Crane. He was president of a large local glass company. He was forty-two years old, six feet one inch tall, and balding. Sounds easy enough, but there was a slight added difficulty to this case in that Mr. Crane had been informed by his attorney that he was being sought as a witness in a superior court civil case going on right now, and that he strongly desired to avoid involvement. He clearly and fully understood that the only way they could command his attendance and testimony was by serving him with a subpoena. Oh, and there was another problem. A few days earlier, a sheriff's deputy had arrived at his company, proudly wearing his full uniform and openly displaying a folded piece of paper in his hands. Deputy Idiot (not his real name) walked into the large corporate headquarters and asked if Mr. Crane was available. Unfortunately, for Deputy Idiot, Mr. Crane's top-floor, dark-glass corner office overlooks the entire parking lot and entryway. Long before Idiot (for short) had even gotten out of his marked police cruiser, Mr. Crane had intercommed his assistant, and she, the receptionist, claimed that Mr. Crane was out of state on business and not due back until late the following week. Mr. Crane chuckled as he leaned back in his high back leather chair and watched Idiot get back in his vehicle and depart. That was easy, he thought.

I got the call when the trial was already in process; it was scheduled to go no longer than three to four days. Aware that Mr. Crane had already been spooked, I knew I had to engage trickery right off the bat. I also knew that I only had one shot or he would slide deeper into protective mode. His attorney may have informed him that Deputy Idiot was the feeble opening act and that another more creative attempt could follow. I needed to factor that into the equation.

Late that afternoon, with subpoena in hand, I drove past the glass company's corporate head-quarters—a very open and well-exposed large three-story building with, as you would expect, lots of glass. The lower level appeared to be made up of retail, wholesale, and fabrication. The dark-glassed upper levels undoubtedly housed the administrative/office aspect and likely my target.

With the commotion of workers departing the facility at the end of their workday, I drove into the parking lot and headed to where the office employees likely parked. Situated next to a side entrance was a large late-model 500 Series Mercedes Benz with a vanity license plate, "GLASS." There wasn't much doubt it was his, and any possible doubt was dispelled by a sign posted on the building in front of the car, which read, "Reserved for Mr. Crane." The distance between the driver's side door and the building door was about eight feet. He wouldn't be outside long. The window of opportunity (no pun intended) was way too small.

This line of work was often a manifestation of odds. I could not help but think that Mr. Crane's office was in the front corner and that he may be able to see his car from his window—there were certainly enough windows.

The next morning, shortly after 10:00 a.m., I drove into the parking lot at a slightly faster than normal parking lot speed. The idea was to project to any casual observer that I was in a hurry. I drove past Mr. Crane's Benz just far enough away from it so as not to allow me clearance for a U-turn. It was always extremely important to know your vehicle—what it could do, and what it could not do. I stopped abruptly and proceeded to reverse my direction by executing a U-turn so that my right front bumper would not quite clear Mr. Crane's right rear corner bumper. At the critical moment just prior to impact, I jammed my brakes enough to jolt my car. I slammed my car into park and jumped out of my car. I slammed my driver's door shut and proceeded to the point of impact with my body blocking any view from the building. *Damn, I'm good,* I thought. My bumper was no more than an inch and a half away from his car...untouched! As I leaned over the fictitious point of impact, I studied the bumper of the Mercedes Benz. After a pause for effect and a look around, I quickly made my way to the entrance reception desk where I explained that I had just hit a Mercedes Benz in the parking lot that had a license plate "GLASS" and I wanted to let the owner know. The receptionist was buying it. Her eyes went big when she realized whose car I had chosen to bruise! I told her that I would be out by the vehicles. I did not want to miss Mr. Crane if he was already engaged as a spectator. I returned and stood slightly leaning over the absence of damage and again blocking any view from the upper-level offices. To add credibility to the "accident scene," I left my car unmoved.

Approximately two minutes later, a man in his forties, fitting the description of Mr. Crane, emerged from the side entrance. I walked toward him and asked, "Mr. Crane, is this your car?" He responded that it was. I quickly interjected, "Mr. Crane, I have some good news and some bad news. The good news is that I did not hit your car; the bad news is that I have this subpoena for you and you are legally served." As I gave him the "bad" news, I extended the paper I had removed from my back pocket.

At that immediate moment of service, a variety of responses can ensue. I've seen everything from someone throwing it back at me or throwing the papers on the ground and stomping on them to just trying to run away. Mr. Crane did none of these, instead he digested what had occurred and let out a chuckle. I think the relief that his prized vehicle was intact was a factor. He seemed amused with the trickery and we ended up conversing for nearly ten minutes. Our meeting culminated in a handshake. After seeing him shortly thereafter at a local bagel shop, we began a friendship that lasted many years.

* * *

As a footnote to subpoena service, whenever I was met with resistance, refusal, or belligerence, I would simply explain that I was an agent of the court and that I was obligated to report my legal service to the judge. Refusal of the presented document or refusal to abide by the subpoena and not show up would result in a warrant for their arrest. I usually had their attention with that bit of information, but frosted the cake with something to the effect that a contempt of court conviction always resulted in fines and a period of incarceration. If possible, I would throw in that the judge on this case was known to be extremely harsh on those he felt disrespected the legal process. With the hundreds of subpoenas I served through the years, I'm proud to say that there was not a single instance of someone failing to appear.

* * *

CHAPTER 14

(MASSAGE) TABLE TURNED

They say the best defense is a good offense. We live in a very litigious society in which attorneys not only encourage people to sue, they also actively solicit by spending millions of dollars in advertising to promote your thinking of "I wanna sue some deep pocket, get rich, and live the dream." It's a modern-day version of ambulance chasing with everybody after everybody. To that end, the mind-set and practice of due diligence has become front and center in the thinking of business and individual liability.

From an investigative standpoint, I was often called upon to not only assist with or execute due diligence, but also to attempt to determine what proactive measures could be undertaken to deter a plaintiff from believing there was liability on behalf of my client. I would work with attorneys as well as loss prevention analysts and actually attempt to conjecture how a jury would perceive situations. The idea that a company or individual took steps to prevent something from happening, greatly lessens the punitive or punishment phase of damages should the harm occur in spite of the attempt to prevent it.

For example, a local dairy that operated a fleet of over a hundred big heavy trucks hired a driver with a horrific driving record. When that driver struck a small child on a bicycle in a quiet residential subdivision, the case against the dairy became immeasurably more valuable when the lawyer for the little girl's family established the truck driver's long history of driving recklessly. "Ladies and gentlemen of the jury (hopefully a jury made up of some parents or grandparents of young children), this business obviously did not care or consider this child's or any child's safety. With reckless disregard, thinking only of getting their product to the consumer, hence, dollars and cents, they put this thirty-thousand-pound deadly weapon into the control of a proven reckless driver, a man with three pages of traffic violations, four accidents, seventeen speeding convictions, two operating under the influence of alcohol, driving to endanger and a total of forty-four other moving violations. Did they check this individual's driving record before hiring him? NO! Could they have spent twelve dollars to get the driving records? YES! What can we do about it today, right now, right here? It's easy… we send a message. We have a unique opportunity today because our legal system CAN work if we do our job. We cannot only decide that this business was wrong in its negligence, but we are allowed to punish them. Our system of justice affords a method to punish the very reckless actions of this business. It's called punitive damages, and the more they pay, the louder the message, not to only this company, but to others watching your message." Although lawyers do it better, I think you get the idea. Had the dairy been able to prove that they practiced due diligence to prevent this type of hire, the punitive damages would likely not even be as serious a factor.

Another case I worked, which exhibits the lack of due diligence, was a nightclub that hired a six foot six, three-hundred-pound bouncer, which in and of itself is not a problem—it's OK to hire a big boy for that kind of position. The problem occurred when this bouncer observed two male patrons pushing each other late one evening. The bouncer proceeded to fly across the room, grab one of the men, and hurl him out a clear glass door that was usually open but not at that moment. The patron's head and body smashed right through it. That flying guy/victim who had been fooling around with his college roommate Rusty will never look the same as a result of the 112 stitches on his head, face, and neck. His lawyer got him close to a million bucks, largely because the bouncer had a lengthy criminal history, documented by twenty-two assaults and aggravated assault convictions. Just like Derek Jeter says in a baseball promotional ad, "I live for this," this bouncer loved to physically abuse his fellow man. The plaintiff's attorney, with the very able assistance of a qualified private investigator to locate them, had several individuals testify that this bouncer had stated to numerous people that he had found his dream job, a place he could legally hurt people and always get away with it!

Beyond the monetary liability typically associated with these matters, the potential for criminal liability sometimes exists.

Within most state's criminal statutes, there are criminal violations specifically directed toward the company executive who egregiously allows the victimization of innocent individuals when related negligence can be determined, exposed, and proven. This calls for serious due diligence.

* * *

This true story was by far my Wednesday night poker group's favorite and usually the one I would pull out at a cocktail party after a few drinks if I felt the audience could handle it. I never had a problem with the male audience; however, a few of the less free-spirited women were not as receptive to the case topic and let their disgust be known with either a verbal or nonverbal reaction.

After a long boring summer day of surveillance with no meaningful activity, I returned to my office to clean up some loose matters, make a few phone calls, and even do a little dreaded report dictation. It was Tuesday, which meant an evening of tennis with Dad and his friends. Playing doubles with guys twice my age was good for my ego…as long as I was on the winning team!

It wasn't a very good night at the net, so I was up for a change of pace, a little something different. My day needed a dose of adventure.

At 9:30 p.m., I parked directly in front of the Improve Your Health Club, located on a very quiet Main Street. With a deep breath and game face on, I walked into the place of business as if I belonged. Opening the door triggered a pair of melodic chimes. No one was going to sneak into this little business. The solid door and darkened windows to the club offered no clue to passersby. Upon entering, one saw nothing other than a six-foot dark gray office partition creating a hallway leaving but one direction to proceed. The lighting was dim and tinted. The air was scented with a soothing aroma of pleasant incense. To the right, I observed a reception-like desk behind which sat a very attractive girl in her twenties with long dark hair parted on the side and falling over her bare tanned shoulder. A low-cut silky lacey blue top revealed enough breast to make me wonder where or if the tan stopped. With her elbows in, her cleavage enhanced, and looking very comfortable in her skin, she exuded sexuality at its very best. With a warm smile, she welcomed me and introduced herself as Candy. I was dying to say my name is Ronald Reagan but didn't want to be too flip. Candy asked me if I had visited the "club" before, to which I responded that this was my first visit, though friends of mine had been here and had highly recommended the place. She smiled again and spoke with confidence, stating that she had never known anyone to leave unsatisfied. Candy then broke into her spiel that she had obviously reiterated a thousand times. I absorbed enough through the distraction of her shiny lip gloss and pretty smile—and did I mention her greatly exposed breasts—to let her know that I would like to have a one-on-one massage session for sixty-five dollars. The brief thought of two girls simultaneously massaging me for a buck twenty struck me as being too distracting. It was also made clear that the girls were primarily compensated with tips for their exceptional services, so I didn't want to spend all my money on the "admission fee"!

Candy told me that I could relax in the lounge with the available ladies for up to a half hour for no extra charge so that I could meet the girls and select the lady of my choice. Complimentary non-alcoholic beverages were available along with gaming tables, comfy couches, and sports events on large flat screen TVs. After a long hard day, this was shaping up to be just what I needed. The thorough enjoyment of anticipation of what lay ahead was seductive in its own right.

After paying Candy and noticing her awareness of my wad of cash, she rose from her seat to expose her lower body—white hot pants, which appeared to have been applied with a paintbrush. I didn't want to stare as she walked in front of me leading me past the partitions; however, if she was wearing anything under those shorts, it was invisible. And she was gliding along on four-inch heels. I think there's a name for those and at that moment, I understood why.

As we entered the lounge area, Candy got the attention of the room by stating, "Hey girls, help me welcome first-time visitor Dave," to which the four girls in the room all responded, "Hi, Dave," "Welcome, Dave," "Nice to meet you, Dave." I nodded and smiled. In addition to the "ladies," two guys in their forties, who were playing pool, casually glanced my way and raised their heads in acknowledgment of my entrance. As I made my way to the juice bar, two of the girls approached the bar as well and arrived there as I did. One of them reached into a cooler and with a very warm smile handed me a chilled glass. She introduced herself as Brittany. As she told me her name, she gave a little half turn, raised her shoulder in a pose-like position, and held it as if to say, "Your move and I'm receptive." I set the glass down on the bar (so I wouldn't drop it) and took a step back to admire her in her entirety. Brittany was a thin blond without much curve to her hips, which were barely noticeable beyond her large D-cup breasts saddled in a tight white halter-top. Although there are times when one wonders, *are they real,* this was not one of those times. I told her she was beautiful, to which she smiled and thanked me. She then made no bones about the fact that if I wanted to see more of her she was ready when I was. For a second, all I could think of was that I was in a poor man's Playboy Mansion and I was Hef!

It was all a little overwhelming, but I managed to meet the girls, taking careful note of their names, or at least what aliases they were going by at work. There was Candy, Brittany, Jenny, Diamond, and Monique. As I nursed my cranberry juice and tonic, I pretended to be interested in a baseball game on an elevated and mounted plasma TV. To the right of the juice bar was a hallway with a silky curtain partially pushed to the side offering not much more than a glimpse of the dimly lit corridor leading to the rear of the "club."

After several minutes of taking it all in, I saw a tall, thin, blond girl emerge from the rear hallway.

Following her was an overweight man in his thirties wearing jeans, a T-shirt, and a black leather vest. I could not hear their parting exchange but it was brief as he departed without looking in any direction except straight ahead. She was my girl, no more than twenty and skin that fit her perfectly (no wrinkles)! I tried my best to be inconspicuous as I checked her out as she checked in with Candy. When she re-entered the room, she made her way to the juice bar. At that moment, the two guys playing pool finished their game and made their move for two girls, Brittany and Monique, who were standing by the couch. A few words and "poof," the four of them disappeared behind the silk curtain. Timing was everything. The two remaining of the four original girls were not for me. My girl, fresh off a session, was the prize of the batch. Just then, the entrance door chimes triggered the entrance of some new arrivals. All I needed was some new competition to whisk away my little blond, leaving me with my half-hour lounge time nearly expired and the two less desirable massage "therapists."

I finished my drink and made my move by slowly but directly approaching my target and introducing myself. It felt like fishing in a stocked pond! We seemed to hit it off!

After the standard name swapping and how are yous, I took the considerate approach. "Hey, Nicole, I know you just finished an appointment, so no rush, but I'd love to be your next client." With a gentle warm touch of my hand with hers, she said, "I'd like that." Then she asked me if I would like to shoot a game of pool first. "I'm not very good at pool but let's play around a little out here and then we can get a room and play a little more," she said, with a tone of flirtation. What a playful little doll. If only my written words could capture her little body language movements, which exuded this "I'm so happy to be me and so happy to be with you" feeling.

It was time for a gift as we approached the pool table. With a smile on my face translated to an invitation to be naughty, I asked Nicole if she knew where the rack was. Without hesitation, she pressed her arms against her sides, pushed out her beautiful breasts, and placed her right index finger on her chin to posture her response, "You don't see a rack anywhere?" We both laughed and then I took her by the hand and said, "My desire to play pool suddenly went away, you ready?" "Yeah," she responded, and left her smiling mouth open for effect. "Besides, I suck at pool and I hate doing things I suck at, let's go."

Hand in hand, Nicole led me to the back area where she entered a small room, dimly lit by a small, rose-tinted lamp on a corner table. The focus of the room was the other piece of furniture, a full-size bed situated in the center of the room and on a frame that made it higher than normal. It certainly wasn't the standard massage table I was accustomed to. There was a water-trickling stone fountain on the table as well as several tubes and plastic bottles of lotions and oils. On the walls were half a dozen small mounted shelves supporting only single unlit candles. And on the last wall was a mounted piece of wood with three clothes hooks. Nicole led me in, released my hand, and told me to get comfortable. "You can hang your clothes right there," she said, pointing to the hooks, "and lie facedown at first," as she peeled back a single top sheet. She then proceeded to light the candles as I slowly unbuttoned my shirt. As she passed the rose-colored lamp, she turned it off, leaving us in candlelight. As I was bent over removing my shoes and pants, she gently placed her hand on my bare shoulder and ran it across my neck to the other shoulder. "I'll be right back," she said with a breathy whisper.

As the door closed, I hurriedly undressed and scooted under the sheet. I briefly questioned myself—did she say faceup or facedown? I was pretty sure she said facedown but wanting to watch her return and since everyone likes a compliment, I propped myself up with one arm and lay sideways.

After too many (probably three or four) minutes, the door opened slowly and in stepped Nicole, the quick-change artist. She was scantily attired in a skimpy red bra out of which she was bursting and a small red patch in her front presumably attached with something I could not see to another small piece of material at the top of the crack of a perfectly round gorgeous tanned ass.

After turning to close and lock the door, Nicole seductively approached me with an inviting smile and the confidence of a champion. I leaned up slightly and could not stop my thoughts as they manifested into a single syllable, "Wow," I said. Nicole guided me down as I turned and lay facedown with my head lying flat wanting to look at this beauty as much as possible. She briefly stood at her workstation, OK table, selecting a dark plastic container and asked if warm lubricating oil would be all right. At that point, she could have suggested 10w40 motor oil and I wouldn't have objected.

A compliment on her "outfit" led Nicole into letting me know that she had come up with this bathing suit design idea with transparent straps giving the illusion of more nudity with very small amounts of material only where legally necessary. She told me that her partners in Florida, where she had just moved from, were working on promoting the concept with designers. I was mildly impressed, but had other things on my mind.

After about ten minutes of probably the worst massage I had ever experienced and some light and meaningless small talk, Nicole shifted gears and went into action. "Since it's your first time, did Candy explain that we work on tips?" to which I quickly put her at ease by telling her that I understood that, and that a good friend of mine had been there before. She seemed pleased not to have to explain her services from square one. Within seconds, Nicole must have wiggled her nose *Bewitched* style or something because in a flash, she was on the bed and straddling my butt as she leaned her upper body against my back and swayed her hair across my head and shoulders. Rhythmically, she ran her hands up and down my thighs and sides, each time edging around the sides of my legs to the front and then separating her warm oiled hands just as they would approach my private area. After a few very enjoyable moments of this, her hands would occasionally stray. She had done this before!

As her intensity increased, Nicole let out an occasional groan as if she was enjoying it as much as I was, which was highly doubtful. She was doing a fine job of making me feel like a man. I let out a few gratifying sighs and let her know how good she was making me feel. Without even asking, she propped herself onto her knees and told me to roll over. As I completed my flip, she was right back on me, noticed my aroused state, and let out an "Oh my!"

Nicole reloaded her massage oil and began stroking me from chest to belly button, stopping slowly and teasingly just at my private zone. After a minute or two of that game, Nicole again reached for the oil, except this time she took my hand and held it out as she squeezed some oil onto my open hand. As she did so, she explained in a sentence the standard tipping for her being nude was twenty dollars, and a hand release like I had never had before was an additional thirty. "Is that OK with you, Dave?" she asked as she smoothly removed her top to expose her beautiful full perky tanned breasts. As I responded in the affirmative, she guided my hands onto her top. She then arched her back and got my hands started at massaging her. "My skin gets dry too! Ohh, that feels sooo good," she groaned. Yes it did, I thought, but it was no time to talk!

Next, Nicole leaned forward again and began to rub her oiled chest against mine. She rhythmically glided up and down, her hair now behind her and my hands on her curvaceous hips guiding her every motion. I lay there with my eyes closed enjoying her every move. Nicole then leaned back, straightening her upper body and straddling her nude lower body across my midsection. With another squirt of oil into her hands, she teasingly asked, "Are you ready for me to massage *everything?*" as she looked at my visible enjoyment and smiled. "Oh yeah" was all I could muster. "I was hoping you would say that" was her response, and Bam! She got onto her side up against me with her head laying on my stomach and my guided arm around her, holding her against me. After completing her first couple of full-length strokes on me, I leaned up a little and asked, "Hey, Nicole, wait a sec…although that feels real nice, what would it cost for, you know, oral?" Resuming a slow sensual stroke of me, she leaned up slightly and apologetically responded, "I'm sorry, but I can't do that; it's illegal and we don't break any laws here. Using my hand is legal so that's all we will do." Not wanting to ruin the moment, I quickly replied, "That's fine… sorry for asking. I didn't know; please don't stop. You feel fantastic." With that behind us, Nicole went to work and performed marvelously!

Nicole finished her handiwork with finesse and then polished the performance with a warm damp cloth. She then gave me another minute of light full body massage and inquired, "Did you enjoy?" I told her she was wonderful as she stood before me smiling. What a doll! Somebody's daughter…I quickly erased that thought from my mind. As she slithered out of the room, she told me she'd be right back. I was putting my final clothes on when she returned, attired in her original outfit. As I was putting on my shoes, she tidied up the room affectionately touching me with every pass.

I removed her tip from my pants pocket, previously counted and prepared, and placed it into her hand. "Thank you, Nicole, I really enjoyed that." With a well-faked "Me too," she told me that she hoped I'd be back to see her. At that point, what is a guy supposed to say? I'll call you! I simply said, "You can count on it." With her job complete and her compensation in hand, Nicole turned the light on, blew out the candles, and escorted me out. I found myself beelining out, not caring to see or be seen by anyone in the lounge. We parted ways at the desk where Candy was seated and smiling. "Thanks, Dave. Please come back and see us again."

"Thanks, I will; good night."

"Now," as Paul Harvey used to say, "for the rest of the story."

I returned to my vehicle and drove off. I reached for my dictation recorder and proceeded to dictate the details of my appointment with Nicole, specifically the exact words stated in response to my request for her services.

Did you think for one moment that this episode was not work? Undercover investigation? A tough job...but someone had to do it.

* * *

This chapter started (though you may have forgotten) with a mundane dissertation about due diligence. There is a connection. The new owner of a chain of massage parlors had recently taken over the business from his brother-in-law, who was now incarcerated—convicted in federal court for prostitution charges. Apparently, some of the girls working for tips had used the "club" as a front to have illegal sex (bigger tips). A jury was convinced that the owner knew exactly what was going on behind closed doors. Despite the defense's attempt to explain that the owner did not benefit from the girls' extracurricular activity, the repetitive testimony of girls describing the evidence suggesting the owners were aware of what was going on resulted in a conviction and a lengthy sentence in federal prison.

It was highlighted by the prosecution team that the owner had hired many girls with prior prostitution convictions and had never done anything along the lines of due diligence in the form of background checks or performance reviews, as was now being performed by yours truly!

Yes, in case you were still wondering, I was getting paid to get naked, get a massage, and attempt to engage these young women in illegal sexual acts beyond what was legally permissible at the time. I had negotiated with the new owner a flat fee of a hundred dollars plus all expenses and tips in exchange for a professional investigator's determination as to whether or not his employees would perform illegal sexual acts. For the record, if a girl had been willing to engage in an illegal act, I was prepared to tell her that I was interested, get her price for the deed, verbally confirm her willingness to perform the specific act, and then proclaim I did not have that much money with me that evening, but would be prepared for that on my next visit. I could then convey my findings within a professionally written report based upon which the owner could terminate that employee and maintain the moral integrity and legality of his establishment.

Although I did not share a lot of my work cases with my Wednesday night poker group, this one was difficult to contain. Not one of them stopped short of volunteering to assist with this matter. They were good friends.

After conducting a half dozen "performance evaluations" at a few of the various club locations, the case took an unforeseeable twist.

One late Friday night, I was standing with my best friend, Larry, at the bar of a popular dance club in the city when he said to me, "Don't look now, but there is a hot girl at a table diagonally behind you and she is locked onto you." I responded that maybe she thinks she knows me. A few seconds later he added, "You're going to find out because she's coming over here right now."

Sure enough, she nestled her way right up to the bar like only a young pretty girl can and seemed determined to get beside me. She was successful. I casually glanced her way and recognized her immediately. Why wouldn't I? Four or five days ago, we had been naked together and she had passed my employment screening examination.

With a discreet whisper voice, she leaned in toward me and said, "Are you working?" Although I had understood every syllable of her question, I responded, "Excuse me?" She quickly elaborated, "Are you working...undercover; I don't want to bother you if you are, but I wanted to ask you something." With a puzzled look, I told her that I didn't know what she was talking about to which she blew me away. "Oh, come on...don't you know? We all knew you were a private investigator testing us. You really didn't know that?"

At that moment, I was stunned. I felt used, slightly embarrassed, and a little cheap that I was a pawn in this scam operation! As a myriad of emotions and thoughts swirled in my head—but trying not to show it—Nicole, or whatever her real name was, explained that she assumed I knew the gig and she didn't want me approaching her saying anything. She was out with a group of friends including a sister who had no idea what she did three nights a week at the "club." "It's the only way I can pay for college and give myself a better life," she apologetically confessed.

I assured her that it was our little secret. She looked very relieved. At that moment, the bartender asked if he could get us anything. I told her that it was probably in reverse order but I politely asked her if she would please let me buy her a drink. She smiled and said thanks. Before returning to her table, she extended her hand, the same one that had held another of my body parts days earlier and said, "Dave, my name is Sharon and it's a pleasure to know you."

"Likewise, Sharon; have a great evening."

"You too, Dave; thanks for being so understanding," she said as she smiled and walked back to her group.

My buddy Larry had bought a couple shots and slid one in front of me. He said, "You look like you could use this right now, who was she?"

I paused, downed the shot, and replied, "Just a girl I used to work with."

* * *

CHAPTER 15

THE BEST DEFENSE IS A GOOD OFFENSE

When a baseball player steps into the batter's box, a series of numbers appear on the television screen. His stats are the criterion for his performance rating. There is the percentage of times he gets a hit in relation to his official number of at bats, along with number of home runs and runs batted in. The pitcher facing him has his own performance criteria, including the all-important win/ loss record. In football, the quarterback is rated by pass completion percentage, among many things, including the all-important win/loss. In fact, we have come to expect and accept people's worth as well as their likelihood for job security, job promotion, and compensation level, all to be directly related to their performance, the win/loss history they create.

I guess I shouldn't have been surprised, but it was an eye-opener to discover that the criminal justice system operated in a similar manner. With parallels to a baseball player trying to move up in the system, my experience revealed and convinced me that prosecutor's advancements are primarily based upon his or her win loss record. The state assistant district attorney likely wants to be the district attorney, and the DA probably has his or her eyes on a federal prosecutor's position, called a U.S. attorney, or maybe the top of the pyramid, a judgeship. I found that this intense competitive desire to get ahead manifested into some hard-to-believe yet easy-to-understand behavior and legal practices.

* * *

When I started working on a federal criminal matter for the attorney of a local businessman, I had no idea what I was getting into. The case seemed rather straightforward at the surface—I'll call him Rudy Catarina, charged with operating and engaging in interstate prostitution.

My client, the defense attorney, Antonio, and I met for not more than an hour. The case was not complicated. The defendant, Rudy, was carrying on a thriving and blossoming business. While it may not be the kind of business that makes your parents proud, nonetheless, it was not illegal to offer and provide a paying consenting patron a session with a scantily clad young lady who would massage and offer a few other "legal" extras for her tip compensation. The "house" would receive the half-hour or hour-long fee paid by the patron in return for providing the facility and to cover the overhead and advertising expenses. The tips they could elicit/seduce from their client once they were behind closed doors generated the girls' only compensation.

If you are reading this with your book club, I hope someone has it figured out by now. There was prostitution going on behind the closed doors. While it was not, at the time, illegal for a girl to disrobe, dance, and provide a hand release (or happy endings, as it is fondly referred to) for a client... for tips, many of the girls were making bigger, much bigger, tips by performing illegal sex acts on paying consenting clients, all behind closed doors. It appeared to be a good gig for everyone involved until some of the "clients" turned out to be undercover law enforcement officials.

This time, it was the FBI. Twice before, the local and then the state police had completely botched the case by entrapment and then going a little too far in the pursuit of evidence! High-paid attorneys defended Rudy, who was starting to feel a little like Teflon. The case had fallen under federal law and jurisdiction when Rudy started delivering girls (just like pizza) and often crossed state lines in his commerce. The feds were much more competent in their work; after all, they were likely promoted through the ranks.

Everything seemed to be insulated. Rudy was raking it in and at the same time providing a safe and clean workplace for the girls who were being handed their clientele. The girls had no problem with Rudy getting his house fee. They were getting every dollar for whatever extras they performed. If a girl had oral sex or intercourse behind closed doors with a big-tipping satisfied customer, the girl retained the entire fee (tip).

By now, the girls were very well trained to question a client carefully in regard to any affiliation with a law enforcement agency. If the undercover cop lied or misrepresented himself, the evidence was tainted and inadmissible. What could go wrong?

Even though the payments from clients were clearly and easily independent of each other, a client generally had a certain total dollar figure he planned on dishing out. When Rudy started overhearing stories of how much money some of the girls were making, he decided to pump up his bottom line. The girls were not too pleased when Rudy nearly doubled the fees a patron was required to pay before he met his "therapist." The impact was immediately noticeable to the girls, who could quickly do the math and see that their fees were being reduced by Rudy's new higher fees. The troops began to get disgruntled.

Rudy was enjoying new profit levels and was getting even cleverer. When a girl was "delivered," the client was charged an additional mileage fee of $.30 per mile. It didn't take long for the girls to learn that the $.17 per mile they were getting paid was just making Rudy fatter and adding salt to the wound. The girls felt they were getting ripped off already, but when Rudy started shaving numbers off miles paid, the stage was set.

Angel was a twenty-one-year-old hot little blond with a two-year-old daughter. The on-again, off-again rocky relationship with her boyfriend and father of the child was well known to the small-town local police where they both resided. Carlos could not stand knowing exactly what Angel was up to. During one of their off-again periods, Carlos had too much to drink one night and confronted Angel. After some yelling, pushing, and shoving, it got more heated. After asking and then demanding that Carlos leave to no avail, Angel called the police. Knowing the police were on their way, Carlos returned home.

A few minutes later, the police knocked on his door and warned Carlos to stay away from Angel—no charges, just a warning at this point.

Carlos wasn't a bad guy. He dearly loved his daughter and was concerned for her safety, especially when Angel was working. He asked the police if he could speak with them for a minute. Carlos explained what Angel did for work and that when she traveled to other states, she left the baby with whatever friends were available. Some of them were well known to Carlos as irresponsible lowlifes incapable of taking care of themselves, never mind his beloved daughter.

State Police Detective Hanson listened to and generally believed Carlos. He had heard of Angel's affiliation with this business. But his ears perked.

"Did you say that Angel traveled to other states?"

"Yes, sir," responded a cooperative and respectful Carlos.

Detective Hanson was friends with some of the buffoons who had blown the case at both the local and state levels. The prosecutors in the DA's office were turning their heads, not wanting to lose again. It was up to the feds and Hanson knew it. The only way justice would be served was by and through the federal system.

With an "informed and reliable source," the FBI was able to get a sting operation put together. They arranged for the engagement of several girls to be delivered out of state to a private bachelor party at which two FBI agents would be mingled. Rooms were wired and discreetly videotaped. Carlos had provided enough detailed information so that specifically requested girls could be hired who would party along with the guys and be willing to earn some big tips. Angel was requested and Carlos had high hopes that criminal charges against her could only help his quest for custody. With big money flying around, the girls loosened up and the FBI agents were able to witness and record money being exchanged for sexual acts.

The discovery revealed no fewer than eight former Rudy girls agreeing to cooperate and testify against their former client-provider. Carlos was invisible.

Revenge time for the girls...oh the wrath!

The girls consistently told federal agents of Rudy's awareness of their sexual activity. They punctuated it with conversations he had with the girls about what certain clients did and liked. Rudy wanted to know, the girls claimed, so that he could better serve the men by knowing their likes and needs and, therefore, better match up the girls based upon those clients' needs. They also made statements and signed affidavits regarding the "training" they received when hired. Those statements revealed that Rudy's wife, Brianna, a working girl, would ask a client if a new girl could job shadow her while she serviced him. From the client's perspective, he was getting a two-on-one, so he generally agreed. During the training session, Rudy's wife and co-owner of the business would engage in either oral sex or intercourse and then explain afterward the different tip rates that went along with the acts. The girls also consistently told how they were encouraged to satisfy the client and that the clients had come to expect sexual services.

The government's case was built solely on the testimony of "the girls." There were no clients willing to step up and testify. Of course, by testifying, they would be confessing to the crime of engaging a prostitute—not a good career move, nor healthy for a relationship.

When a case had no physical evidence, it became a case of credibility. It would boil down to a defendant's word vs. the eight girls. Interestingly enough, the statements made by the girls all had some common elements and seemed suspiciously similar. I sensed that the federal investigators might be putting something in the girl's mouths beyond what the girls were accustomed to—words.

Within hours of my investigation, I discovered that the defense would rely on the character of the girls. Of the eight girls, three had prior convictions for engaging in prostitution. I realized immediately that this could backfire. Using due diligence, an owner could have easily determined this and prevented the former prostitutes from being hired. Four of the girls, all under the age of twenty-six (several under twenty) had children, though none were married. Most importantly, all of the girls had pending prostitution charges stemming from the incident, which resulted in Rudy

Catarina being charged. To varying degrees, all of the federal witnesses could be cross-examined and made to look less than desirable to a jury. The federal prosecutor would talk to the theory that it was the government's job to get the big fish and to do that, you had to go through this process of nailing the smaller fish.

The mountain to climb was that there were eight prosecution witnesses and even though they had a bruised past, it was difficult not to believe that much of what they were saying was true.

To get a better feel (no pun intended) for the case, I conducted interviews with several of the working girls that were still employed by Rudy. I'm not sure I have ever experienced a poorer exhibition of coached testimony. No matter what I asked, the same scripted response was provided. "We are told not to do anything illegal; if a client requests a sexual act, we tell them we do not do that and ask them to kindly leave and that their fee will be refunded," and on and on.

I saw some investigative value in confirming and further detailing the reasons why some of the girls were disgruntled. I couldn't help but think what a greedy moron Rudy was. He was making gobs of money but wanted gobs plus a little extra at the expense of his moneymakers, the girls. They turned on him, and it didn't look pretty for Rudy now that the competent feds were involved.

Private Investigation 101 would have led me to interview the eight girls, starting with those not quite as involved, in hopes of building a line of inquiry for the key prosecution witnesses. Instead, I decided to go right for the kingpin, Angel. I knocked on the door to the townhouse-style condo, the last known address for Angel, but to my surprise, and very good luck, Carlos, the inform- ant, greeted me.

Carlos was more than willing to talk and I was a great listener. He asked a lot of questions of which I answered none. His recent and self-serving cooper- ation with federal agents did not erase the years of his distrust of law enforcement. He was fascinated by my role and the fact that my job was to keep the law enforcement people honest. Justifiably, all Carlos cared about was his daughter. His hope was that after a prostitution conviction against Angel, he could make his case for custody. Carlos's con- cern stemmed from the rumor mill that Angel was telling people that none of the charges against her would stick.

I left Carlos, knowing full well that the feds were playing a high-stakes game of *Let's Make A Deal.*

A check of court records on the eight girls revealed that although all the prosecution witnesses had current pending criminal charges, none of them had trial dates; in fact, there were no procedural dates set in the system. It was becoming clear. While it is very common for prosecutors to make deals by offering immunity and/or lesser charges in exchange for testimony against a bigger fish, it is typically done aboveboard. Those deals are legal because charges are filed against an individual and a jury would be made aware that the witness is testifying in exchange for consideration. The defense can then argue that the deal taints credibility as the prosecutor explains to the judge and jury that, despite the negotiations, the testimony is truthful. It is standard operating procedure. It happens all the time. It is part of the fabric of the criminal justice system. There is nothing wrong with it.

In this case, I had Angel saying that nothing would stick. She seemed pretty confident, as if she knew something. I also had a bunch of girls who had a lot at risk, including their kids.

I located Leslie Probert and identified myself as a private investigator. Without giving her a chance to say a thing, I continued by explaining that I had just a few questions regarding her statement in a criminal matter and that it would only take a couple minutes. She immediately keyed in on my role, "Are you working for Rudy?"

Despite my Ford LTD and blue blazer, she could see right through me!

It wasn't the first time I had faced this query. "I'm not working *for* Rudy. He is not paying me and I'm not trying to get anybody off. His attorney, who basically is trying to figure things out, hired me because he can't do that sitting on his ass behind his big desk. So the attorney hired me to find out the truth. Leslie, I'm just looking to find out the truth."

At this point, I often had 'em, but if I didn't, I might let them know that most of the time I do my job properly, the case pleads out, and no one ever has to testify. That was a convincing incentive to review what they already had said. I would let the witness see what I had in my possession, which was his or her statement on some official-looking letterhead.

If any hesitation remained, I might throw in an, "I would think you'd want to know what the lawyer was going to ask you prior to having to respond in a public arena." And if all else failed and they still didn't want to talk, I'd pull out my last ditch effort.

"I understand and if I were in your shoes I might be leery to speak to me too. I'll tell you what, you don't have to say a word or answer anything you don't want to, but let me tell you what the attorney is trying to confirm. It might even give you a heads up as to what you are going to get asked if this case goes to court, which I'm hoping we can avoid."

In all the years and the thousands of interviews I conducted, I truly cannot recall anybody disallowing the dialogue to continue at this point.

If it got to the latter strategy, the idea was to break their silence. I would do some easy basic review, which may get an occasional nod or a body language confirmation. Then I would look for a benign error along the lines of their age or even middle initial. Perhaps someone by the same name with a different middle initial who had a tainted past was brought up and the witness would clarify that she was not that person. A sincere thank you for straightening that out and relief as to what that may have caused, a comment about how it was a good thing that we're doing this, and usually we were off to the races. Most people want to tell their side of the story; especially if they know the other side has been told.

In the federal case against Rudy Catarina, my goal was to make sure that there was an even playing field and that the truth, and nothing but the truth, was revealed.

Back to Leslie. After a little reluctance to speak with me, Leslie began to loosen up. She was amazed that I knew all about the details of how Rudy had begun to skim the girls' profits.

"What a scumbag, huh?" as I lured Leslie in to a comfort level.

After listening to her robotically tell her story, I began to sound like I was wrapping it up. Then I delivered the blow.

"Leslie, you seem like a nice girl who has been thrust into this mess. And I've seen a lot of shit come down when the stakes are high like this in the criminal justice system. The only advice I want to give you, and whether you take it or not is entirely up to you, is to please make sure that you have your deal in writing. I've seen so many cops lie to people through the years. They tell you one thing and then it's your word against theirs and whom do you think the judge is going to believe? But you have a lawyer, right?"

"No, they said I didn't need one." Leslie responded, now all of a sudden thinking of only her own ass.

"Holy shit!" I exclaimed. "They don't give a flying fuck about you, Leslie. I know about this so-called deal and, quite frankly, you're going to get screwed if you aren't careful. Don't you see? The cops don't want you to have a lawyer because this deal they are offering isn't real. A cop can't make a deal, only a prosecutor or a judge can do that. They're going to use you for their own purposes and then they'll disappear. I know about the deal, Leslie, be careful."

With an aura of serious concern, Leslie let it fly. "How do you know about the deal?" After the appearance of a struggle as to whether I should disclose, I lowered my voice to a near whisper and said, "Angel told me."

Leslie immediately responded that it was supposed to be a secret to which I snapped back, "Don't be a fool, Leslie. Can't you see that they want it to be a secret because it's not real and it's not legal? Do you want to trust your future to a cop who tells you to keep it secret?"

By now, I had Leslie in the palm of my hand. I simply suggested she get an attorney who could get this "fictitious deal" confirmed and in writing. I gave her my card and told her she could call me anytime at all to talk or bounce things off me.

I had to move on. I had a bigger fish to fry.

Within an hour, I was with Angel. After the same initial reaction of skepticism, I broke down the barrier by dropping the fake deal card. The line that broke her was, "I suppose you believed them when they told you they would stop the Department of Human Services from taking your daughter? Angel, the FBI has no jurisdiction over DHS. Unless your attorney has this deal in writing, you have nothing. Oh, wait a minute, I almost forgot, they told you that you don't need an attorney (playing on my recent Leslie findings)."

Angel was a firecracker, especially when it came to her two-year-old daughter.

All I wanted was the truth and I was going to be damned if the truth was going to be tainted by obtaining statements under false pretense.

I felt I had pierced the veil of the prosecution as I suggested to Angel that she simply get an attorney to protect herself and her daughter.

Feeling pretty good that I had at least begun to penetrate the feds' tactics, I hopped in my car and headed back to my office. As I turned into my parking lot, some twenty minutes later, my cell phone rang. It was my client, Rudy Catarina's attorney, screaming into the phone.

"What the hell did you just do? I just got a call from the United States Attorney's Office threatening to charge you with all sorts of shit. What's going on?"

"Hey, hey, calm down. They're just pissed that I broke down their witnesses and got them to talk when the FBI had told them not to say anything. I think I'll have some good stuff before we're done."

"Well, according to them, you're done now. They're talking about going to the federal grand jury and charging you with multiple counts of tampering with a witness and obstruction of justice. David, they sound serious. They are wild."

"Listen, Antonio, I'm not stupid. I knew this could get dicey so I brought along another private investigator with me who witnessed the entire thing. They can't get me for something I didn't do."

Or could they?

I knew what they were thinking. It was elementary at this point. The best defense was a good offense. And what better offense than the arm of the law, the federal law with FBI agents and the professionalism of the federal criminal justice system. These were the best of the best, which in my mind, translated into the sleaziest of the sleaziest, the most corrupt of the most corrupt, the ones that felt more than anyone else in law enforcement that they were above the law and how dare anybody challenge their supreme authority. In my opinion, they were as bad, if not worse, than any criminal I had ever encountered.

A few days later, the FBI was knocking on my door looking to interview me regarding an investigation of allegations that I had threatened witnesses in a federal case and that I was attempting to obstruct justice. With a great deal of disrespect, I declined their request for an interview feeling so proud of myself that I had covered my ass by hiring another PI to accompany me.

To make matters worse, the case was assigned to an aggressive and brilliant prosecutor from the U.S. attorney's office who in my opinion had this matter blown out of proportion in his mind.

The prosecutor flexed his muscles and got word to me via Antonio that he would be presenting evidence to a grand jury to get me indicted.

Still not concerned but thinking that I should at least confirm and document the truth, I revisited both Leslie and Angel. After several days of no returned telephone calls and them not answering the door despite obviously being at home, I got letters from their respective attorneys—"Stay Away!" Well, at least they took my advice on getting an attorney, I thought. However, it was clear that they had been swayed back by the feds and they were now against me. Unbelievable, I thought to myself—once a whore, always a whore. The feds were powerful and I was certain that in the face of exposure, they were working diligently to smoke-screen their behavior by focusing on attacking me. Thank goodness I had brought a fellow PI with me, good old Jack.

I decided to pop in on Jack and get up to date with him. I wondered if the FBI had tried to talk with him. As I turned into his office parking lot, I was glad to see his car present, an old beat-up sports car, but nonetheless, a sports car. Jack liked playing the stereotypical *Magnum P.I.* role.

As I entered the office, I encountered his receptionist/assistant, Melinda. Jack burst out of his office and blew right by me, barely speaking and proclaiming an emergency.

"You need help, Jack?" I yelled as he departed.

"No, all set."

Before I could say a word, Melinda exclaimed, "Yeah right, emergency...pussy alert."

I wasn't feeling too good about how this visit was playing out.

I engaged Melinda in a conversation, assuring her my strictest confidence. Luckily, we had become pretty good friends ever since I introduced her to my buddy Larry one Friday night when we were all out drinking away our stress. Melinda knew what was going on and she elaborated on her calling her boss a pussy.

"There was no emergency; he saw you coming and bolted because he feels so guilty."

Now, this was getting very uncomfortable.

"See these roses?" Melinda asked. "You know who they're from?"

With a perplexed look, I responded, "Larry?"

It broke the tension and took the edge off the situation.

"No, they're from Jack! He was so happy this morning after returning from a meeting with the FBI, that he bought me flowers."

"You're shittin' me!" I blurted out.

"David, I wish I was. He is such an asshole. The feds pressured him and he caved. They threatened to either press charges against him as a coconspirator or cooperate and face nothing. He told 'em what they wanted to hear and now he actually believes it. He said you were kind of rough on the girls when you were interviewing them. He also told the FBI agents that he was there during the interviews but that he didn't say a word. He's been on cloud nine all day now that they have backed off him."

"Melinda, thank you. I swear I won't say a word but that helps me a ton knowing what I'm up against. We never spoke."

"Good luck, Dave," she said with all the sincerity in the world.

"Thanks, Melinda. I'm OK."

I drove off in a daze trying to figure out how this all unfolded. I catch the FBI making illegal deals with witnesses, and the next thing you know, I'm the criminal. Not only do they have the two girls saying that I committed these crimes, but now they make a deal with my associate. I remember saying it out loud as I drove away, "Let's Make a Fucking Deal."

I wanted so badly to communicate with this asshole prosecutor at the U.S. attorney's office but I knew it would be a mistake. Despite the fact that I had done nothing wrong, the reality was that I was in deep shit. The same words I had spoken so many times to people who had been sucked into the criminal justice system resonated in my mind.

"It didn't matter what had actually happened or what the truth was, it was a matter of what could be proved or in this matter, disproved." And once some loser cop or prosecutor decides whom they want, they could rationalize nearly anything as a means to that end. If it means overlooking evidence that contradicts their direction, no problem—destroy or ignore it. If it means creating evidence or putting words into people's mouths— no problem. If they need something that doesn't exist—no problem. They could create a charge or threaten their powers, make a deal, and presto… they have what they want. It happens every day and the more "they" get away with it, the more likely it will continue in epidemic proportion. I understand how and why they get to that point but, fundamentally, it is so wrong. In my opinion, these people undermine the judicial system and extract the fairness and rights bestowed upon us by our Constitution. The problem is exacerbated by the fact that there is virtually no degree of law enforcement...over law enforcement. In many ways, it's like the Wild West. It is out of control.

As much as I wanted to avoid the expense of hiring a lawyer, my need for representation was high. Thankfully, I knew a little bit about retaining an attorney and the utmost importance in hiring the right one. My needs in an attorney included someone with experience dealing with federal laws and someone who was experienced dealing with the tactics and abilities of the federal prosecutors within the United States attorney's office.

I interviewed four or five prospects in order to obtain what I considered the most important piece of my defense. One attorney told me that he "knew the game down there" (at the feds) and was experienced in federal criminal cases. I quickly responded with a follow-up question. "Name the people you know or have dealt with at the U.S. attorney's office."

He couldn't name one person. I told him he was wasting both of our time, picked up my stuff, and walked out. I didn't need an attorney desperate to collect a retainer who would learn on the job. The stakes were high, my freedom. I wasn't going to make my first mistake be my demise.

I eventually hired a thirty-eight-year-old woman who specialized in federal criminal cases—Lauren Olsen. She was a former federal prosecutor in Pennsylvania. Before I left her office, she had blasted out a letter informing the feds of her representation of me and warning them not to try to contact me. I was feeling better already.

Not only do the wheels of justice spin slowly, the wheels of injustice are just as slow. Many weeks went by with very little activity. I monitored the federal grand jury indictments, waiting to see my name on the esteemed list. My attorney kept the FBI off my back.

On a hot August afternoon, about two months before the Catarina trial would begin, the feds surfaced. The FBI was blowing this case out of proportion. It was conveyed to my attorney that all charges against me would be dropped if I would connect the defendant to his organized crime contacts from out of state. Although this was a small town, petty criminal matter, the FBI wanted to believe they were busting the mob!

First of all, I couldn't connect him even if I wanted to because there was no connection. And if there had been a connection, I would be a bigger fool to be the one to connect the dots.

My attorney snapped back that the offer to drop charges was a joke because there were no legitimate charges. The feds didn't like that and talked about getting an indictment and that they would hold onto the indictment until hold onto the indictment until Friday, September 13, and arrest me late that afternoon. By doing so, I could spend the weekend in jail before getting out on bail that next Monday. Then he chuckled about knowing my plans for September 14, which was the day I was getting married.

Once again, I was amazed how I could possibly face this humiliation after doing nothing wrong other than holding the FBI accountable for their actions. Even though I knew I was and would be found innocent if the case ever got to a jury, I didn't need the perception of being indicted by a federal grand jury. As it was, my soon-to-be in-laws weren't too crazy about me!

Even though we denied the connection to any type of organized crime, the feds never really believed that there was no involvement. They finally resolved to leave me alone as long as I didn't testify in Catarina's case. With all previous negotiations aside, I was informed through my attorney that IF I testified, I would be arrested as I stepped out of the courtroom and face criminal charges that could be punishable by up to five years in prison. Catarina's attorney, Antonio, was brought up to speed and sympathetically asked me what I wanted to do. I didn't hesitate.

"Put me on the witness list; I'm telling my story."

I got married on September 14, without incident. In the back of my mind, I was envisioning federal agents showing up and hauling me off as I screamed, "I do."

With the trial in process, I sat in the ornate marble halls of the federal building, waiting for my name to be called. I was ready and actually looking forward to the exchange I would soon have with the federal prosecutor. Many hours passed with very little hallway activity. There were four FBI agents hanging around and pacing the halls. A few were stone faced but a couple of them would exchange hellos or casual nods.

Something I will never forget occurred on the third day of trial. I had departed the men's room and was walking down this long corridor as I observed an agent approaching me. In light of our previous casual exchanges, I offered a friendly, "How you doing?" as he neared. He never stopped, but when he was very close to me, he slowed down and said, "You did the right thing," and kept walking. I may never know the true meaning of his comment; but I have an idea that he was referring to my unwillingness to connect the dots...dots they still believed existed but dots that I will always deny knowing anything about, even if I did.

On day five, the courthouse security locked the courtroom doors in preparation of the judge "charging" the jury. This occurs after both sides have rested their respective cases and the case is ready to go to deliberation. The doors are locked and no one is allowed to enter or exit during what can be as long as an hour process. I was in shock. How could the case be handed to the jury when I hadn't had my day in court?

The next thing I knew, the courtroom emptied. I approached Antonio and gave him a bewildered look. "What happened?" I asked.

"I don't think it would have made a difference and it would have opened a can of worms. We didn't need the jury thinking we were trying to intimidate the witnesses." As he walked away, he had great difficulty looking me in the eye.

Even though I was off the hook, I didn't feel good about it. I felt like our side caved in to the threats and intimidation of the feds. I also will always wonder if the feds had actually threatened Antonio, the defense attorney. Words he had used in an earlier conversation led me to believe this. He had referred to his potential liability based upon my actions. Sure enough, my not backing down likely shifted the threats to Antonio. I couldn't call myself as a witness, so they got to him. I can hear it now.

"You call Smaha and we focus on him working as an agent for you, Antonio." The feds knew how to exert their influence and they are quite intimidating. They usually get their way. They are the supreme bully!

Rudy was found guilty and, honestly, that was most likely the correct verdict. The travesty was that the wrongdoings of the FBI were never revealed and the fact that they got away with this impropriety only serves to encourage that continued behavior.

The "girls" all walked and probably continue to walk...the streets.

* * *

CHAPTER 16

CLEAN

One of the most common responses to telling someone that you are a private investigator is being asked about hiding in bushes trying to catch a cheating spouse. I never enjoyed disappointing people, but I could count on one hand the number of domestic cases I worked through the years. Although largely by choice, a no-fault divorce state made findings in that regard completely worthless. I typically discouraged inquiring callers, advising them that they likely already knew what was going on without throwing good money at an already bad situation.

One of the very few domestic cases I recall working was obligatory. An insurance adjuster client with whom I had developed a long and lucrative work history asked me for a favor. I was asked if I would speak with her brother. All she had said was that he suspected his wife was up to something. What was I to do? "Of course," I responded, "I'd be more than happy to talk with him and see if I can help."

Bernie called me fifteen minutes later and, after identifying himself as my client's brother, proceeded to spew his woes. He barely took a breath during his rambling several-minute dissertation, the gist of which was that he was convinced his wife was having an affair. She had been going out three nights a week with her "girlfriends." Bernie and his wife had two kids who were fourteen and sixteen so they required very little care. There was a pattern to her activity, he explained. She worked from 7:00 a.m. until 3:00 p.m. at a local food manufacturing facility. After getting home, she would spend a few hours with the kids and her husband and then shower and go out at 5:30 p.m. to meet her friends for a quick bite or a salad and a little girl time. Bernie went on to say that she didn't return home until after midnight, at which time she would proceed directly to the basement and remove her clothing in the laundry room. After slipping into a nightgown, Rosemary would slide into bed where Bernie was either sound asleep or at least pretending to be asleep. The alarm would go off at 6:15 a.m. and after stirring the kids, she was out the door at 6:45 a.m. in order to punch in by 7:00 a.m.

On a couple of these late-night jaunts, Bernie questioned his wife's late-night return, but was met with only vague responses which had a tone of *that was your final question.* I asked what type of explanation she offered for her time away and he told me that she would simply claim to be at a girlfriend's home chatting or playing a game. Bernie didn't buy it and frankly, based upon the limited and one-sided information I had, neither did I...and he had not even played his best card. Two nights ago, after pretending to be asleep upon her return, he waited for her to fall asleep and crept to the basement. The clothes she had worn were placed in the washing machine but the load was not run. He explained that the washing machine running often caused the old piping in the house to rattle and he presumed she did not want to awaken him for potential questioning. Anyway, upon removing her sexy pink underwear, much to his dismay, he discovered they were very wet. He couldn't stand it any longer. It was eating him up. It was all he thought about during every waking hour and it was causing more waking hours than he wanted. With a grand finale tone he blurted out, "How much would it cost me to nail her? I want photos so she can't deny it."

I slowly and carefully attempted to explain to Bernie that it was not always that easy and that it can be very costly. Usually when someone is up to something for which they do not want to get caught, they become very suspicious and an investigator can lose a subject. On and on I went trying to discourage my involvement. Then I realized that a typical human nature response kicked in. It seems like the more you try to turn someone away, whether you are selling them, dating them, or trying to avoid being hired by them, the more they want "it" or you!

Bernie wasn't biting, "I'm hoping I don't need to spend a lot of money because things are tight; I'm out of work and the bills don't stop." I explained that surveillance is very expensive and not always fruitful. I can usually tell by the way someone drives and the frequency of their mirror use whether they are suspicious of being followed. If they are, it is common to tag team the subject with radio communication between surveillance vehicles. I felt compelled to explain to my future client that I'd rather lose someone I am trailing and have the opportunity to resume on another date then get made and virtually obliterate any hope of a successful result.

After throwing every ounce of "you really don't want to do this" persuasion, Bernie had other ideas. I think he had been watching a lot of television, including the daytime dramas. He asked if I had the ability of testing the panties. "Can you test 'em to see if there is any semen in the panties?"

Having the resources of a laboratory was a necessity. Seeing a potentially easy way out, I quickly responded, "Of course we can." Bernie was thrilled, "Great, that's what I want to do, how much would that cost?"

"Let's see (pretending to look it up), the lab I use charges ninety dollars (actually sixty) so I'll do it for you for a hundred bucks total." If I could lose this guy, avoid surveillance, appease his need to do something and not alienate his sister, my good client, for short money, I would consider it a major victory.

Bernie knew her schedule. She would be going out this evening and returning to remove her clothing in the early morning hours. He would wait until she was sound asleep and retrieve the panties. At this point, I interjected that he replace them in the washing machine with another similar pair and that he place the panties to be tested in a ziplock bag. "Of course," he replied...silly me for suggesting!

Right on schedule, Bernie turned into our designated meeting spot. He parked next to my vehicle, driver's side to driver's side so we were within a couple feet of each other without having to get out of our vehicles. Bernie was similar to how I had imagined, a big guy with a matching gut, probably in his late forties, though looking all of midfifties. His hair was unkempt and he had misplaced or even lost his razor.

I lowered my window and gave him a low-key, this-is–all-business, "Good morning, Bernie." "Are you Dave?" was his reply. My thought was *No, I'm just a guy you've never seen before driving a car meeting the exact description of the one you were told to meet who happens to know your name, you stupid fuck.* Immediately realizing that Bernie was getting right into his participation in this entire undercover private investigation gig, I responded in a low discreet voice without turning my head, "Affirmative." With that, Bernie proceeded to hand over to me a crumpled lunch-sized brown paper bag. I took it from him, set it down on my passenger seat, and waited for the second phase of the encounter, an envelope with a hundred bucks, cash. I had explained to him that the cash method was simply to protect him. He got it! With that complete, I told him that I should be back to him in a couple days. These tests can take a little time.

As I drove off, I checked my envelope and found that in order. Next, I slowly peeked into the bag hoping like hell that Bernie had followed my instructions. Sure enough, pink lacey panties safely sealed in a ziplock bag. I could only imagine that Bernie had a busy day ahead of him made up mostly of daytime TV and attempting to harness his imagination. At that moment, I would have bet ten to one that at some point before this ordeal was over, Bernie would make inquiry expressing an interest in working as a PI.

Although I had every intention of delivering the panties to the lab, I knew the testing was not time sensitive. I got busy on another case and never made it to the lab that day. So when my weekly poker group convened at my house that evening and asked if I needed help with any of my cases (see chapter 14), I couldn't help but let them in on the panty testing. The peanut gallery chirped in, "For a hundred bucks, give 'em to me. I can tell; I have my ways," and even Dick the "pig" of the group said, "I'll sniff 'em for nothing." Then the talk went to depositing semen on them to make sure the client got what he was looking for and the brains of the group, Larry, offered, "What if the guy she's banging wears a condom?" Even the peanut gallery could hit a nail with a hammer once in a while. The panties made their way around the table with my insistence that the ziplock bag not be opened. *I need new friends*, I thought to myself.

The next morning, I delivered the panties to my friends at Matthews Laboratory and by midafternoon I got the call from my buddy Pat, "Negative, no evidence of seminal fluid." At that moment, you can't help but wonder about your client's reaction. Would Bernie be happy and relieved or disappointed with the findings? The result certainly did not resolve the suspicion and offer closure. Even my card playing buddies could see one of the potential loopholes...the mystery man could be wearing a condom!

Bernie took the news in stride almost as if he anticipated the result of the test. He had obviously perceived the likelihood of the findings and lack of resolution because even though he was financially strapped and unemployed, Bernie immediately asked what I needed to initiate following her. The good news was the end-of-the-day pattern with which I could work. After agreeing on a quarter of what I would typically take for a retainer, I told him to meet me two days later, same meeting spot, this time with a photo of his wife; the year, make, and model of her car; and names and addresses of possible friends with whom she may be socializing. The meeting also gave me the opportunity to return the panties to him and make him pay me in advance, which might even, with a little luck, make him change his mind on conducting the surveillance.

Equipped with long-range telephoto photography capability, as well as nighttime video and audio equipment, and even my new toy—night vision gear—I set up surveillance approximately twenty minutes prior to Rosemary's patterned departure time. I was dreading this!

Right on schedule, the beat-up black Isuzu SUV emerged from the dead-end street being operated by a female driver. It proceeded at a moderate to fast pace along a well-traveled thoroughfare and then onto Interstate 295. I was on the ramp, two vehicles behind her and feeling very much inconspicuous. This girl was not out for a casual ride. She was driving with a destination and wasn't wasting any time in getting there. After a couple of miles, she ramped off the highway and headed toward the downtown district.

Knowing the downtown/port area to be configured like a peninsula and being extremely familiar with it, following her was easy using parallel streets and catching only brief glimpses of her vehicle's rear end. Based upon her direction and the lay of the area, she was likely not too far from her destination. Feeling confident that she had no clue as to my following her, I closed in a little tighter. Within a minute, she turned into a dead-end narrow entryway that I knew led to the back of a large office building and ran parallel to a street full of bars, clubs, and restaurants. She could easily park behind the building and take one of several paths to the strip. I opted to proceed past where she had turned into and headed down to the happy hour busy strip of pubs. After parking my vehicle illegally (I had friends at Parking Enforcement), I walked briskly up a paved throughway that emerged onto the area where I presumed she was headed. Sure enough, there was her vehicle, parked at 5:55 p.m. in a premium parking spot marked, "Reserved for Mr. Boynton," a bank officer I presumed. No sight of Rosemary. There was no way she had hoofed down to club alley. I had lost sight of her for a matter of two minutes but it sure seemed likely that she had entered the rear entrance to the bank. A casual walk past the glass-door entrance revealed a night guard one would have to walk past in order to get anywhere within the eighteen-story office building. I maintained surveillance and observed only the occasional office worker departing and walking toward one of the three nearby parking garages.

Maybe she was banging some bank executive who had a job, wore nice clothes, treated her nicely, and actually shaved. In addition to the bank and its headquarters, the building also contained law firms, investment companies, and a variety of other businesses capable of paying the costs of the high-rent district. I had only an hour into it so I decided to maintain surveillance. It was very easy to inconspicuously maintain a vantage point that afforded a view of Rosemary's vehicle, the door to the office building, and the general area.

After a couple hours of inactivity, the day's light was fading. Now I was committed to determine what was going on. With a baseball game on the radio and my cell phone affording me the opportunity to check in with some friends, I opted to stay put.

After a couple hours and with nothing observed relative to Rosemary, I decided to take a little walk around the area. It was as much to stretch as anything. I strolled down the street on which all the bars and restaurants are located and peeked into most of them, seeing no one even closely resembling my girl. As I walked back toward the office building, I was shocked as I looked up. In the fifth-floor window, there was Rosemary. Up and down, up and down, up and down…went her arm as she vigorously cleaned the large window. A minute later, she was doing the same thing to the next window and the next. *Holy shit*, I thought. She's cleaning at night to earn some extra money while her unemployed husband sits home spending whatever little money the family has on an investigator. Rosemary was busting her sweaty ass trying to make ends meet. The panties were wet all right, with perspiration! I would later learn from my insurance adjuster client that her sister-in-law went out at night using the pretext of harmless girl time so as not to bruise the already fragile male ego of her husband, Bernie. What a shmuck!

And if you took the ten to one odds, you lost. "Hey," he uttered, "one good thing came out of this. I was wonderin' if you had any openings. I think I'd be pretty good at it."

As much as I wanted to chastise him on the "one good thing" line, I decided it best not to. Instead, I politely explained the difficult educational/work experience/testing criteria as administered by the state in order to become licensed as a private investigator.

"Got a pen? Here's the number," knowing I would never have to speak with him again.

* * *

CHAPTER 17

ONE, TWO, THREE FOR THE ROAD

I always enjoyed the innovative or creative defense strategy while all along being fully cognoscente of the fine line between real and creative. It is truly a fine line.

As you read this story, imagine yourself serving on a jury where you would decide between guilty or not guilty.

* * *

Rick Walker was charged with operating under the influence. The prosecutor systematically and methodically paraded witnesses onto the stand. The arresting police officer testified and was followed by the state toxicologist, who testified that Mr. Walker's blood alcohol content was .11 or three-hundredths over the legal limit of .08—pretty straightforward, huh?

Rick Walker got stopped at 10:20 p.m. after he quickly pulled out of a local drinking establishment parking lot, apparently not seeing the oncoming vehicle, which just so happened to be a police car. He likely wouldn't have seen it even IF Walker had remembered to turn his headlights on. Naturally, the vehicle gained the attention of Officer Buchanon who immediately pulled Rick over.

After getting pulled over, Rick was questioned and acknowledged that he had had a few drinks, adding that he was fine to drive. The strong odor of alcohol combined with a driving blunder provided probable cause, allowing Officer Buchanon to test Rick's blood alcohol level. Rick politely requested and was granted permission to telephone his wife so that she would not worry about his not showing up, as she was expecting him any second. Rick then stated his refusal to take a Breathalyzer test because of his belief that the test was not as accurate as an actual blood test. He stated that he was willing to have a blood sample taken and politely requested that means of testing. Rick would later admit to me that he had made this request in an attempt to delay testing in hopes that he could get a lower level by stalling as many minutes as he could.

Due to a small uprising at the local county jail requiring all available officers to assist, combined with an 11:00 p.m. shift change, Walker's blood was not taken until 11:15 p.m., nearly an hour from the time he was stopped. Walker was sitting there, thinking he was a genius!

Rick's blood alcohol content came back at .11 and he was subsequently charged with operating under the influence. Bail was set at $100 cash.

Rick waited for his wife to arrive with his bail and pick him up. Ironically, she was late, taking a lot longer to get there than what he expected.

The state's star witness, the state toxicologist would now become a defense witness...after the defense attorney laid some groundwork. First, the jury would hear a series of five credible witnesses who would testify that they had been with Rick Walker the evening he was stopped. A jury would hear that just before Rick left the bar that evening, he downed a shot of Jack Daniels whiskey and chased it with two 14-ounce beers that sat before him. His "friends" had told him that he couldn't leave until he finished what had been purchased for him. It would simply be rude. The witnesses testified that they knew his wife was agitated and that she had called him two or three times on his cell phone. In an escape mode, Rick consumed the shot and the beer, grabbed his coat, and bolted.

I had interviewed the state toxicologist at length, which paved the way for the defense attorney to begin his questioning with confidence. The expert witness, as determined by the state during their case, testified that alcohol takes time to get into the blood stream. Depending upon body type, the body's digestive status, and the rate at which each individual metabolizes, the alcohol generally takes between forty and sixty minutes to show up in one's blood.

"In other words," Mr. State Lab Toxicologist, "based upon the premise of Rick's consumption already established, it is highly likely that approximately ten minutes after the surge consumption by Rick, his blood alcohol content was significantly lower than when his blood was drawn fifty minutes later?"

After a little haggling over the word "significant" and the confusion that other previously consumed alcohol would have further metabolized and lowered a test result, the bottom line equated to the "expert's" scientific opinion being offered. Based upon the scenario presented, the test could have yielded a blood alcohol result of three-hundredths lower had Rick Walker's blood been tested immediately or at the time he was actually operating his motor vehicle. The underlying beauty of the case was this: how could the state prosecutor discredit his own expert? The prosecutor regularly relied upon testimony from this witness to obtain convictions.

Closing arguments were straightforward by the prosecutor. Most prosecutors, in my opinion, had a very difficult time thinking outside the box. On the other hand, the defense attorney hammered home the details of the alleged crime. There was credible evidence, including cell phone records, which corroborated the pre-driving circumstances. Then it came down to the nitty-gritty detail of "what was Rick's blood alcohol content when he was driving?" Arguably and based upon the state toxicologist, the BAC could have been as much as .04 lower at that time, putting Rick just below the legal limit of .08. Throw in a margin of error of a couple of hundredths and how could one be certain, beyond a reasonable doubt, that Rick was actually above the legal limit when operating his vehicle?

A sympathetic jury of his peers found Rick Walker not guilty, a jury carefully chosen and primarily made up of married men. As the jury was being screened, we had a belief that many married men would relate to the portion of the defense involving peer pressure at the bar and trying to get away from your friends to avoid the wrath of the waiting wife.

* * *

For what it is worth, at the writing of this case, it is nearly fifteen years from when I investigated this matter. I did not then nor do I now advocate defending any operation of a motor vehicle by someone under the influence of alcohol. I do not recommend any attempt to profess a defense along these lines after drinking. I do not advocate drinking and driving or the use of technicalities to avoid taking responsibility for your actions. In this matter, we were dealt a hand and the facts revealed a sequence of events that led to looking at the law from an angle one may describe as "outside the box." Simply put from a defense perspective, was the defendant ever operating a vehicle with a blood alcohol content over the legal limit? I don't think you can say beyond a reasonable doubt that he was. At the very least, I think it provides for good cocktail party discussion!

* * *

CHAPTER 18

AND IN THE END...(BEATLES)

My greatest client; my most memorable case...

It was a bitter cold January night when Dan was awakened in the early morning hours by a grand mal seizure. He had been the profound "picture of health" at sixty-nine years young, an avid and competitive tennis player, and strong skier. He took pride in his undeniable ability to keep up with his sons at challenging mountain peaks throughout the Rockies to the infamous Tuckerman's Ravine at Mount Washington in New Hampshire.

To all who knew him, it was a shock and a brutal wake-up call that a malignant brain tumor can occur to anyone at anytime.

Dan's second wife, Ethel, took all the proper steps, keeping him as calm as possible while awaiting the arrival of the ambulance. Her volunteer emergency medical technician training and work may never have been more valuable.

En route to the hospital, Ethel placed a telephone call to Dan's only local son, Brian, who knew immediately that something was wrong when the phone rang at 2:00 a.m. He rushed to the hospital and met them in the emergency room. Not a lot was known other than everyone felt an overtone of fear.

After a series of tests, the worst of the worst fears were realized—the diagnosis that the seizure was caused by a brain tumor.

The doctor, a general practitioner and lifelong friend of Dan's was there at 4:00 a.m. to convey the bleak news to Ethel and Brian. Tests revealed a sizeable area of abnormal growth that had triggered the body's neurological response of a seizure.

Ethel held one of Dan's hands while Brian held his father's other hand, as Dr. Covel explained to his childhood friend the unfortunate grim findings.

Dan's eyes swelled up and he trembled slightly as he attempted to hold back the tears. He eventually succumbed to the emotion and through his controlled tears said, "I need to make peace with Derek." Ethel and Brian knew what he was referring to.

Derek was the oldest of Dan's three sons and resided in Arizona. Several months earlier, he had written his father a scathing but brutally honest letter, calling it the way he and his brothers saw it relating to the "second wife syndrome." You know, the one that has played out thousands of times where the second wife attempts to alienate her new husband from his past life, which means coming between the father and his children. They usually start out appearing to want to all get along, but when the new wife gets her place established, she manipulates the division. It is very easy to understand, yet very difficult, if not impossible, to prevent.

In this particular case, as is likely typical, you had a financially comfortable man "starting a new life" with a woman who had nothing, whose kids had nothing, yet she was bound and determined to turn that around and quickly, all the while professing over and over that money was not important. It was her version of the American Dream. It's never too late to climb the socioeconomic ladder but at this stage of life, you better realize that the most likely route is to do it on the back of another.

The letter sent by Derek spelled out Ethel's "transparent to everyone else" ways. It provided a logical case with many examples evidencing her self-serving actions with his money, which had created and continued to inflict financial stress and a financial burden he had worked his entire conservative life to prevent in preparation for his golden years. And although it may have felt good to write and deliver the message, it fell on a man who had been worked on and manipulated in preparation for the potential of a backlash of this sort. Besides, she was with him every day and had fostered a codependency that would not compete with an opponent three thousand miles away. In a convoluted way, once the division was confirmed, it played into her scheme perfectly. In her eyes, it was one down and two to go.

The next few days were a whirlwind, not only emotionally but logistically as well. After a difficult procedural brain biopsy, which required drilling through the skull, the family sought out the so-called experts. Several meetings with local neurologists resulted in a recommendation to pursue a higher standard. It was believed locally that the best hope for Dan was Boston, Massachusetts, specifically a protocol treatment at Tuft's Medical Center, which was being conducted by a team of highly regarded brain cancer experts who were targeting this specific type of oligodendroglioma tumors. The local neurologist spoke of very positive results being reported, though cautioned that the program was relatively new, cutting edge, and there are always risks. The family ignored the latter part like the standard dissertation of risks you hear every day on pharmaceutical ads on TV.

The neurologist sensed the optimism on the faces of Dan and his family as he delivered the caveat. Not everybody was accepted into this treatment program. The process began with the local neurologist presenting the profile to the Tufts team and then, upon passing the initial screening, the patient would spend the better part of a day in Boston being tested and evaluated for acceptance.

Even at the earliest stage of the process and feeling nearly hopeless, it was clear that the success of the treatment and, thus, the fame and recognition to the doctors who discovered the elusive "cure," was a numbers game. The team of doctors, all fantasizing about their photos on the cover of the *American Journal of Medicine* holding their golden award, would be selective regarding participants. They didn't want a failing specimen candidate who was already too far gone. That would hurt the numbers. Instead, deliver them a "healthy" version of a human with this tumor, who would be more likely to withstand the effects of treatment and potentially survive a little longer. The family didn't care about who got credit and what the motive was; to them it was about the precious life of a dearly loved man.

The family pledged their entirety to do whatever necessary to get Dan accepted into this special treatment program.

With a subdued undercurrent of hope and cautious optimism, the family would wait to hear. Dr. Hallick, the local neurologist, had agreed to submit Dan's profile and medical data to his colleague, the head guy at Tufts. The ball was in their court. It was now a waiting game, which, in the family's minds, was literally a matter of life or death.

The next afternoon, as if God had answered their collective prayers, Dr. Hallick called and delivered the welcomed news. Dr. Benson, the head honcho, numero uno guy of this protocol treatment, wanted to meet the following day at his office in the Tuft's Medical Center at 9:00 a.m.

Brian would not sleep well that night because of the same feeling when you know you have to catch an early morning flight. No matter how many alarms you set, you still seem to witness every hour pass on your bedside clock.

At 6:00 a.m. sharp, he picked up his father and Ethel and off they went with over an hour of cushion time. There are certain things in life you don't want to be late for and this was at the very top of the list.

Shortly after 9:00 a.m., Dan, Ethel, and Brian were escorted into a very large modern office within the hospital. It was more than a little shocking that such an expansive and impressive space even existed in the hospital. It more closely resembled the office one would imagine being the workplace of a CEO of a major corporation. Not lost in the moment was the fact that these three visitors were being hosted in the valued space.

Seated behind a magnificent ornate desk was Dr. Malcolm Benson, a forty-plus-year-old thin man with even thinner hair. The well-dressed doctor broke his eye contact with the medical file in front of him and stood to greet the three with a warm and welcoming handshake. After initial introductions, he gestured them toward a conference table where three other doctors, one male and two females, were standing and awaiting the arrival of the patient and his entourage.

Each doctor took a turn explaining his or her respective area of specialty in treating brain tumors. There was a laser radiation, chemotherapy, and an extraction surgery "expert" at the table; however, each of them concluded their presentation with a diagnosis that due to location or proximity to sensitive areas, their treatment method was simply not feasible in this case. Dan, Ethel, and Brian listened intently and occasionally, politely inserted questions for clarification purposes. The mood was somber but at the same time, they knew they were there with a purpose. Patience was the necessary ingredient to the equation.

At the conclusion of the specialists' dissertations, Dr. Benson immediately began. "I know it sounds like nothing but negative news, but allow me to offer an alternative that, in my opinion, is extremely exciting." Having heard nothing but gloom and doom, the prospect of something "extremely exciting" was welcome to the ears. The patient and his entourage collectively sat up and moved a little closer to the edge of their seats. The room was silent. No one wanted to delay the information about to be offered.

Dr. Benson knew he had a captive audience as he described his new potential breakthrough treatment that was specifically designed for this exact condition. Although he cautioned that the treatment was in its infancy trial stages, he explained that an air of cautious optimism existed, based upon documented results with lab animals and early indications in humans. And as if an angel had appeared in the room, Dr. Benson, this very man sitting across from them, was the lead doctor of this new program...their very own Dr. Benson.

Having always exhibited a tendency for impatience and never more so than now, Dan exclaimed, "Let's do it."

Enjoying the limelight and knowing exactly where he stood, Dr. Benson upped the ante by describing the process used to qualify accepted applicants. Brian resisted his inclination to say, "Name your price; everything has a price. Let's hear it. What's it going to take?" Instead, he shut his mouth and was surprised at what he heard. There was no cost to the program. If the patient passed a comprehensive physical examination and was willing to sign a stack of medical forms and disclosures, the treatments, thus the hope, began. Treatment consisted of a daily injection of their concoction, which worked its magic by passing through the patient's bloodstream and zeroing in on only those cancerous cells it detected. The formula had been shown not to necessarily kill existing cancerous cells as much as inhibit and prevent those cells from duplicating and spreading. In addition to the injection, the patient would take a dose of other known and established drugs to strengthen the immune system, including steroids to prevent swelling. The swelling of the tumor had caused the initial bodily reaction of the grand mal seizure. It all sounded like it made perfect sense.

The next hour epitomized the expression of "signing your life away" as Dan rifled through documents merely looking for the signature lines so he could get to the next one. He actually got to the point where he brought an element of levity to the situation as he signed and stated, "I have no fucking idea what I'm signing but I don't really care if I can get this (treatment) going."

Dan was scheduled for his physical that afternoon at 1:00 p.m., affording a brief time for lunch. The mood at lunch was magically optimistic.

At 4:15 p.m., the entire group reconvened in the elaborate office where they had first met merely seven hours earlier. It was no surprise as the various doctors verbalized the positive results from the physical examination, but with the stakes so high, enthusiasm was contained. When the results and scores were delivered, the room grew silent.

Dr. Benson knew the ball was in his court as everyone anxiously awaited his verdict. He removed his reading glasses and began, "You are all such nice people. And that makes it even more pleasant for me to say this to you. We feel that you are a perfect candidate. If you still feel like you did this morning, I extend to you our most heartfelt welcome to our program.

That was it. All the cool, calm, and collectivity were out the window. Like the enthusiasm following the final out of the final game of a World Series victory, the family exclaimed a simultaneous exultation of celebration with hugs and a few tears to boot. It was a very special feeling and moment in time.

After the dispersing of the first injection and oral medications was administered, Dan and Ethel reviewed a detailed printout of all the instructions. Weekly appointments were set for Wednesday mornings at 9:00 a.m. To the delight of everyone, the injections were tiny needles and nearly painless, as the needle was pricked into a pinched layer of a love handle. It was all good.

Winter turned to spring and with the change of season, new hope for life blossomed. Weekly trips to Boston had become a gladly accepted ritual. The treatment certainly seemed to be serving its intended purpose. Seizures were nonexistent and life was cautiously getting back to a degree of normalcy. Dan was given the green light to drive again, having gone over four months seizure free. The day Dan drove into his son Brian's driveway was a day of celebration. They embraced and, without saying a word, a volume of emotions raged. It was all good.

As an "experimental treatment patient," aka a guinea pig, Dan was occasionally subjected to the medical aspects of the program. In a nutshell, this meant that medication dosages would be tweaked in an attempt to ascertain the most beneficial levels to minimize side effects and at the same time effectuate desired results. With Dan doing so well and all test results (and there were plenty of them) returning positively, he was a prime candidate for

experimentation. One such medication modifica-
tion caused a serious rash in late August.

For the first time, there was a setback. Every
square inch of Dan's skin was red and irritated.
The incessant scratching, itching, and pain caused
not only a physical complication but a psychologi-
cal blow as well. Dan could not sleep and the stress
mounted. Nearly daily trips to Boston were made
in an urgent attempt to regulate the treatment
and get back to pre-rash status.

After three horrific weeks, the irritation subsided, but tempers had flared and things had been
said that could not be taken back. Ethel had clearly
grown tired and worn out from the caretaker role.
She persistently verbalized her disdain for the treatment program and lobbied for its termination.
Ethel lobbied for a new approach. "Why don't we
just enjoy whatever time we have left and forget all
the medication?" She had so persistently badgered
and promoted her position to Dan that he would
not object, "just to shut her up." But he made it very
clear to his children and everybody else that he had
a lot to live for and that he wanted to fight on.

In an apparent statement of rebellion, Ethel
was now unable to make all of the trips to Boston.

It was very clear that she preferred to discontinue the treatment.

In another statement, she claimed that she could no longer provide the level of care that Dan required. Enter private nurse, Sherry.

For Dan, quality of living turned on a dime. It was good again. Sherry was not only a nurse but she became a great friend, conversationalist, and as if that was not enough...she loved to cook, and excelled at it. What a match. Dan loved to eat and was profoundly appreciative of the masterpieces Sherry would create.

Even Ethel embraced the arrival of Sherry and the role she filled so well. It afforded her the freedom and flexibility to live her life without the burden of being caretaker. Her schedule filled quickly with clubs and socials within the community... away from home.

Although Brian found Sherry initially a little cold, it didn't matter. He knew the absolute joy she brought to his father. His daily visits were also a little more comfortable, as he would arrange them to coincide with Ethel's ever-growing social commitments.

This journey of life was cruising along and everyone seemed to have adjusted quite well. Brian, a new father of a baby girl, would bring the baby over several times a week, bringing utter joy to Dan, the new grandfather. Ethel seemed to be "just heading out" nearly every time Brian arrived, which was just fine for everybody.

As the Christmas holiday approached, plans were made for Brian's two brothers to come to town. This did not sit well with Ethel. She protested that Dan was not up for company and that the stress could trigger problems. To Dan, life was about family. He was thrilled to know that he could be together with his boys. "What a perfect gift," he would repeatedly exclaim.

"I think you're making a mistake, a big mistake," Ethel would mutter, as she would dramatically storm out of the house as Brian arrived carrying his new infant.

The next evening, Brian arrived shortly after 7:00 p.m. to find Ethel not heading out for the night. She appeared upset and asked to speak with Brian alone in the kitchen before he saw his Dad, who was asleep in the living room. Ethel wanted to prepare Brian for what could be a difficult realization. She proceeded to tell Brian that Dan had awakened that morning very confused and disoriented. He was not doing well and she was very concerned. Brian listened as he peered at Ethel, who noticeably could not look him in the eyes.

That night, Dan slept. Ethel suggested Brian call her before his visits to make sure his father was awake. "No sense in you just sitting here and watching him sleep...that way he gets to know you're here. He looks so forward to your visits." Brian kissed his Dad's forehead and departed... feeling very sick in the gut.

The next morning Brian called Ethel only to be told that Dan had been awake most of the night but then had a big breakfast at 5:00 a.m. and was now sound asleep. She suggested he try calling later that afternoon.

That afternoon, Brian called again. Ethel told Brian that his father was awake but not feeling well. According to Ethel, he had asked if he could have the day to recuperate and put off a visit until the next day. It felt very, very uncomfortable.

The next morning at 8:30, Brian's cell phone rang. Not recognizing the number of the incoming call, he answered, "Hi, this is Brian." It was his dad's nurse, Sherry, and he could tell something was wrong before she had finished identifying herself. He listened intently, suspecting it was not going to be good. He was right yet totally off base as to the content of the "bad news."

With a quivering emotional tone, Sherry unloaded. "Brian, I have never in my thirty years of personal nursing become involved in family matters, but I can't hold this in any longer. I need to tell you about some things that are going on."

In the same vein in which a suicide hotline operator would want to keep a caller engaged and on the line, Brian tried to put Sherry at ease. "It's OK, Sherry, take your time, take a deep breath, and let's talk; it will be OK."

Sherry appreciated the comfort. "I am so sorry. I need to apologize to you and I am so sorry. Ethel had told me so many awful things about you and your brothers and I believed her. Now I know how untrue it all was and I see how wonderful you are and how close you all are to your dad. I love your father so much. He is so special. But I wasn't very nice to you boys because I bought her shit. Brian, we have to do something. I heard her tell you last night and again this morning that your dad was asleep or wasn't up for company and it's not true. He was awake and wondering where you were. He lives day-to-day looking forward to your visits. He's been very disoriented lately as if he is not getting his medication. I started listening to Ethel when she didn't know I could hear her. I used the baby monitor Ethel borrowed from you by hiding it under the bed."

Sherry took a deep breath and then burst into tears as she told Brian, "That bitch told your father this morning that you had not been to visit him in three weeks and your father cried like a baby."

Not wanting to break the flow of information coming from Sherry, Brian restrained comment but felt rage like he had never ever come close to experiencing in his lifetime.

Sherry continued by telling Brian that Ethel had removed photos of him and his brothers that had been around his bed and replaced them with photographs of her family. That was enough. Brian was on his way to see his dad. It was agreed upon that their conversation "never took place."

When Brian entered his father's house, he had to resist grabbing Ethel by the throat and pinning her against the wall. He wanted to destroy the bitch but realized that would cause more harm than good, especially in terms of his father's well-being. There would be a way…there would be a time…he had to believe that.

He hugged his dad, a little tighter and longer than normal.

Ethel offered to give them some privacy and said she was going to take a walk.

As soon as she left, Sherry rushed into the room with her finger to her lips and pointed to the baby monitor under the coffee table. Privacy hell. Ethel had the receiver with her and was just outside around the garage, well within range to hear every word exchanged. However, she wouldn't. After a couple warm friendly exchanges, Brian took the Brookstone massager and clearly announced that he was going to give his dad a shoulder massage. "Let's see, I can plug it in right here, oh, I can unplug this," after which Ethel would hear nothing but an earful of static and only believe its disconnection was an unfortunate sequence of events.

Before Brian could settle in, his father asked him when he had last visited. Brian told his father that he had been there the day before yesterday and that the only reason he didn't visit the previous day was that Ethel had told him that he was not feeling like company.

In a rare and selective use of vulgarity, Dan responded with emotion, "That fucking bitch, she told me you hadn't been here in three weeks.

I didn't say anything but I didn't believe her. Why would she do that?" And then Dan let it be known that he knew the answer to his own question though he didn't state it.

He took a deep breath and then said, "We need to talk about this."

Sherry added, "Yes, you do."

With that confirmation, Dan got noticeably stronger in his failing condition. "I need to make sure I'm getting my medication."

At that point, the front door flew open. Ethel was back. She wasn't about to let them talk without her ear in the room.

Brian quickly stated that tomorrow night is Ethel's Garden Club meeting. We'll get to the bottom of this.

Ethel barged into the room stating that it was too cold to walk and plopped her ass on the couch. She glanced at the unplugged monitor to confirm her static source. So much for her offer of "privacy."

The next night could not have come soon enough for any of the three. Brian had called Ethel to say that he was not feeling well. He would not be visiting that evening. He certainly didn't want to introduce germs into his father's fragile system.

To cement "act one," he asked to speak with his dad so he could say hi and explain that he'd be by as soon as this scratchy throat passed. Dan played along and seemed to love the game. Everyone with the sensitivity to whatever was going on felt Brian's absence would ensure that Ethel departed for the evening.

Sherry made sure that Dan had all his medication that morning and that afternoon as well. He was going to be alert that evening. She knew that it was imperative.

The "secret" meeting was implicitly called to order upon Brian's arrival. No one quite knew in what direction it would go but there was something amiss and they all wanted to get to the bottom of it. Ethel's suspicious behavior was telegraphing something that had to be figured out.

Dan took the lead without mincing his words. "What the fuck is going on and what is she up to?" and before there was a sliver of time to answer, he added, "I don't trust her, she's up to something." He supported his belief by referring to the fact that she was always whispering and always taking phone calls in the other room, behind closed doors.

Nothing was solved or resolved that evening other than the realization that something had to be done. There was a bond forged among Dan, his son, and his caretaker, all of whom had a profound "need to know" what was going on. They also had come to realize that time was of the essence and the services of a professional investigator were necessary to succeed in this mission.

My investigation was initiated at this stage of events. After considerable thought and discussion, Dan loved my proposal. Tap your very own telephone line. Chances were pretty strong that if Ethel was leaving the room and whispering a lot, conversations were taking place that she didn't want others to hear. And there had to be a reason she didn't want others to hear what she was saying. No need to speculate when you will likely get it from the horse's mouth.

The wiretap and recording equipment were delivered the next morning. Not that it mattered, but the question was posed, "Is this legal?" Dan responded, "What are they going to do…throw me in jail?"

In a matter of thirty minutes, the equipment was installed in the basement behind a rarely used workbench. The tape would be activated upon the line becoming live and would record twelve hours of material. It was agreed upon that Dan would monitor the tape and, when it neared completion, it would be swapped out with a new tape, and the first tape would be reviewed.

Dan was enthusiastic about the prospect of outsmarting his self-proclaimed "clever" wife.

Two days later, Dan called and said it was time. He handed me a tape and said, "It's full." I swapped him for a blank tape and told him I'd give the tape a listen the following day while on surveillance.

With a big appreciative smile, he said, "I wouldn't want to be you!" I must have had a questioning look on my face because he felt compelled to explain. "I can't stand listening to her for five minutes and now you have to listen to her for the better part of twelve straight hours!"

I couldn't wait until the next day. Late that night I put on my headphones and hit play.

As an investigator, you become acutely aware of people's behavior and actions. They say that actions speak louder than words, but I will tell you, from all my experience, there is nothing and I mean nothing more powerful and revealing than hearing someone's own voice and in their own words incriminating themselves.

It didn't take long. Ninety minutes into the tape, Ethel was heard speaking to another unidentified female. A sick feeling overcame me as I propped myself up in bed and listened intently. The feelings that something was amiss were validated. Ethel was speaking in a hushed voice and commented that she needed to be careful. She didn't trust anyone, including the nurse. She told the woman with whom she was speaking that everything was right on schedule.

Before turning the tape off at 3:00 a.m., I had learned that someone named Jay was supposed to be visiting that Friday which would have been the next day. In addition, Ethel made several disparaging comments about Dan's boys, that they would be shocked to see their father's condition. She suggested that he would not even know they were there, and then added, with an evil chuckle, that they all "think they can walk on water." There was bitterness all right but the degree with which it would manifest itself was yet to be clearly defined.

The next evening's visit by Brian was not productive, as Dan slept soundly from 6:00 p.m. through the night. Ethel attributed his condition to having had a lot of company that day. "It was nonstop," she barked. Actually, there was only one visitor, according to Sherry, and that was Jay. Ethel dismissed Sherry early as an act of "kindness." That left Jay and Ethel alone with Dan.

Thankfully, Ethel was going to be away the next evening, affording the group an opportunity to reconvene.

It was determined that Jay was a lifelong friend...of Ethel's and just so happened to be an estate attorney. Dan vaguely recalled the fact that Jay had recently visited, but could barely recall a thing about the visit. He commented that he was not having a coherent day. A light bulb went off above everybody's head. No words needed to be spoken.

Then Dan blurted out, "I signed papers. He told me he was updating my paperwork. I have no idea what I signed. Oh dear God." By now, he was very emotional but even more determined.

Over the course of the next two weeks and dozens of hours of telephone call monitoring, it was determined that Ethel had redone Dan's will and yes, very much to the benefit of her and to the near exclusion of Dan's children. They were left in the will by just a trace, which was strategically described as more likely to hold up in a court proceeding.

Also revealed within the tape-recorded calls was that Ethel had a secret wall safe installed in her residence.

Ethel became aware that Brian, at Dan's request, had removed Dan's briefcase from the residence for a day. Dan explained to Ethel that he wanted Brian to have a copy of his papers.

Within twenty-four hours after that tense exchange involving Brian's removal of the briefcase for "copying" purposes, Dan took an extreme and sudden turn for the worse. The seizures returned; the disorientation was extreme, and tests revealed a surge in tumor growth that was out of control. He became comatose.

I removed the recording equipment and tape from the basement. It found a home on a bookshelf in my office.

Dan passed away peacefully a few days later with Brian at his side.

The funeral was a wonderful tribute to an amazing man. Dan's three sons all eulogized their father with loving heartfelt words. In the final tribute, Brian briefly referred to the love he and his brothers shared with their Dad and how nothing or nobody could ever get between that strong loving bond, no matter how hard she tried. He paused and glanced Ethel's way as she sat isolated surrounded only by her children.

Dan was gone but his last words were yet to be conveyed.

Brian's attorney contacted the estate attorney, Jeff Greenberg, who was an associate in the same firm as Ethel's friend, Jay. Both Brian and Ethel were named as executors so they would both be present at the reading of the will. Jeff seemed a little taken aback that Brian had retained an attorney but obliged to accommodate the meeting.

The next afternoon at 1:00 p.m., Brian entered the law firm accompanied by his attorney, Danton Sturgis. They were seated in a conference room.

Ten minutes later, Ethel and Jeff entered the room—no sign of Jay, who was likely hiding out back. The attorneys were cordial. Ethel quickly took a seat with her eyes cast downward. Brian stared at her, refusing to acknowledge anyone.

Feeling the chill, Greenberg didn't mince words.

"OK, let's get to it. I have been provided by Daniel's attorney with a very recently dated will, I would request permission to read Daniel's last will and testament."

Danton Sturgis politely invited him to proceed.

It was unbelievable. Basically, everything left to Ethel with the exception of a small yearly stipend to the boys and that was left to Ethel's discretion.

At the conclusion of the reading, Greenberg stated that it was clearly what Dan wanted. It was dated a mere ten days earlier. Ethel looked up slightly and nodded.

As if to validate the "ten day" comment, Sturgis inquired, "What was the date on that, Jeff?"

"January 18," he responded.

In Columbo-style fashion, Sturgis fumbled through his leather briefcase and removed some papers. He adjusted his reading glasses as he slowly focused on the final page. Attorneys don't often get a chance to live out movie-style legal drama so Sturgis was extracting all he could out of the moment.

He tossed the papers onto the table as if revealing his royal straight flush at a poker tournament. "I believe you will find this version of Daniel's intentions to be a little more current."

There was an immediate outburst by Greenberg in which he stated he had never seen such an atrocity. Ethel stood, and in shock stated that there was absolutely no way that the offered document could be valid. Translated, based on later obtained information, I believe she meant, "After Dan signed my version of the will, he was never coherent again because he wasn't getting his medication." Maybe he didn't get his medication after her version was signed...at least not from her.

After a few nasty words directed at Brian by Greenberg, Brian responded. "I think you will find that my Dad's most recent will is exactly the same as the will he has had for years. It takes care of and provides well for that bitch. It truly honors his intentions. Unlike most, he was a man of honor and it gave him great departing pride to right the incredulous wrong that your client, that despicable human being right there, attempted to manipulate. She's not as clever as she thinks. And the only thing that will make this ending more satisfying will be," as he glared at the bitch, "if you dare challenge Dad's intentions and the entire truth is revealed. Hope to see you in court."

Brian and Sturgis departed, leaving a stunned pair to figure it all out.

Despite threats of legal challenges, they never materialized. Ethel was clearly defeated. She failed. She caved. Perhaps she was not quite as clever as she had professed so many times.

Before her lawyer threw in the towel, we had determined that the "grieving widow" had rushed to the bank minutes after her husband's body was removed from the house by the funeral home. The irrefutable purpose of the visit, which was captured on bank surveillance cameras and then documented by power of attorney executed documents, was to cash in certificates of deposit despite having to incur early withdrawal penalties. There was no mystery as to her sense of urgency. The POA would expire after the date of death and she was obviously aware of that detail.

As an investigator, there is no means to a successful result unless you inject passion into the equation. I think it is true about nearly everything in life. My passion to help people allowed me to enjoy every aspect of my investigation work. The passion I incorporate is partly the manifestation of truly caring and the indescribable satisfaction to right a wrong. Just because my investigative role may conclude or a client's needs are satisfied, and just because I was paid and could easily move on to a waiting matter, it does not necessarily mean I am done. I seek closure for personal gratification.

Several months after Dan's death, I guess I was ready. I looked at the tape in the recorder and noticed that it was nearly full. Rewind...play.

What I heard will never leave my memory. As I listened, I concluded that it was no accident that Dan deteriorated so rapidly in the days following the newly executed "Ethel will." The doctors knew what they were saying when they described Dan's medications as a matter of life and death. My final question can be answered only by speculation. I often wonder what verdict a jury would have returned on a charge of murder against Ethel... if the tapes were admissible evidence in a court of law. I believe she would have spent the rest of her life incarcerated.

* * *

The End

www.ingramcontent.com/pod-product-compliance
Lightning Source LLC
Chambersburg PA
CBHW062124280526
45788CB00001B/44